# THE DIGITAL PROJECTS PLAYBOOK

A Step-by-Step Guide to Empowering Students as Creators

GRADES 3–12

## JOHN ARTHUR

Copyright © 2025 by Solution Tree Press

Materials appearing here are copyrighted. With one exception, all rights are reserved. Readers may reproduce only those pages marked "Reproducible." Otherwise, no part of this book may be reproduced or transmitted in any form or by any means (electronic, photocopying, recording, or otherwise) without prior written permission of the publisher.

555 North Morton Street
Bloomington, IN 47404
800.733.6786 (toll free) / 812.336.7700
FAX: 812.336.7790
email: info@SolutionTree.com
SolutionTree.com

Visit **go.SolutionTree.com/technology** to download the free reproducibles in this book.

Printed in the United States of America

**Solution Tree**
Jeffrey C. Jones, CEO
Edmund M. Ackerman, President

**Solution Tree Press**
*President and Publisher:* Douglas M. Rife
*Associate Publishers:* Todd Brakke and Kendra Slayton
*Editorial Director:* Laurel Hecker
*Art Director:* Rian Anderson
*Copy Chief:* Jessi Finn
*Senior Production Editor:* Suzanne Kraszewski
*Copy Editor:* Jessica Starr
*Proofreader:* Charlotte Jones
*Text and Cover Designer:* Abigail Bowen
*Acquisitions Editors:* Carol Collins and Hilary Goff
*Content Development Specialist:* Amy Rubenstein
*Associate Editors:* Sarah Ludwig and Elijah Oates
*Editorial Assistant:* Anne Marie Watkins

Dedicated to my students, the 9th Evermore.
Your light shines so brightly.

# ACKNOWLEDGMENTS

**TEACHERS RARELY GET THE** chance to publicly thank the big-hearted humans who have helped make their dreams come true. So, like an Oscar winner taking the stage, I'd like to take this opportunity to thank the following people, without whom I could never have written this book.

- Stacey, my remarkable wife, for making all things possible
- Ione and Valentine, my wonderful daughters, for always inviting me to play (even if I'm not as fun as Bluey's daddy)
- Suka, Alan, and Christin Arthur—my parents and sweet sister—for not laughing when I said I wanted to be an elementary school teacher
- The incredible parents who trust me with their children's education
- Mrs. Kathy Anderson, my inspiration, for once saying I should be a teacher
- Heidi Green and Maggie Cummings, my principals, for always encouraging me to do what I know in my heart is right for my students
- Keenan Burkley, Tom Luthy, Tyler Schultz, Christine Gibbs, and Sarah Keady for being the best teammates I have ever had
- The entire community at Meadowlark Elementary School and the Salt Lake City School District for their endless love and support
- Juliana Urtubey, for helping me center community wellness, joy, and justice in my students' creative works
- Last, but certainly not least, my extraordinary acquisitions editor Hilary Goff, who found me in the wild and transformed me into a published author

Solution Tree Press would like to thank the following reviewers:

Doug Crowley
Assistant Principal
DeForest Area High School
DeForest, Wisconsin

Teresa Kinley
Secondary School
Humanities Teacher
Calgary, Alberta, Canada

Jennifer Renegar
Data & Assessment Specialist
Republic School District
Republic, Missouri

Visit **go.SolutionTree.com/technology** to download the free reproducibles in this book.

# TABLE OF CONTENTS

*Reproducibles are in italics.*

**About the Author** .................................................. xi

**Preface** ............................................................ 1

**Introduction** ....................................................... 3
    The Benefits of Digital Projects .................................... 4
    Empowering Student Voices .......................................... 6
    Engaging Parents and School Leaders ................................ 6
    How to Use This Book .............................................. 10

### PART I
**Digital Voices** .................................................... 11

### CHAPTER 1
**Digital Voices 101** ................................................ 13
    Benefits of Blogging, Presentations, and Podcasts ................. 14
    Online Research, Media Literacy, and Artificial Intelligence ...... 17
    Digital Tools and Technology Tips ................................. 25
    Amplifying Student Voices ......................................... 29
    Conclusion ........................................................ 32

### CHAPTER 2
**Blog Posts** ........................................................ 33
    Creators at Work .................................................. 33

The Project.......................................................................36

Conclusion........................................................................43

CHAPTER 3

**Presentations**..................................................................**45**

Creators at Work...............................................................45

The Project.......................................................................49

Conclusion........................................................................58

CHAPTER 4

**Podcasts**........................................................................**61**

Creators at Work............................................................... 61

The Project.......................................................................64

Conclusion........................................................................74

PART II

**Digital Videos**................................................................**75**

CHAPTER 5

**Digital Videos 101**..........................................................**77**

The Benefits of Video Production.......................................77

Film School......................................................................79

Amplifying Student Voices: Online Video-Sharing Platforms..............102

Conclusion......................................................................104

CHAPTER 6

**Documentary Short Films**..............................................**105**

Creators at Work.............................................................105

The Project.....................................................................108

Conclusion......................................................................120

CHAPTER 7

**Narrative Short Films**....................................................**121**

Creators at Work.............................................................121

The Project.....................................................................124

Conclusion......................................................................133

**CHAPTER 8**

**Music Videos** .................................................... **135**
    Creators at Work .............................................. 135
    The Project ..................................................... 138
    Conclusion. ..................................................... 150

**Epilogue** ......................................................... **153**

**Appendix** ........................................................ **155**
    *Five Fascinating Facts Form* ................................ *156*
    *Critical Friend Feedback Form* ............................. *157*
    *After-Project Reflection* ..................................... *158*

**References and Resources.** ................................. **159**

**Index** ............................................................. **163**

# ABOUT THE AUTHOR

**JOHN ARTHUR** teaches sixth grade at Meadowlark Elementary, a Title I school in Salt Lake City, Utah. Since 2013, his students have gained national recognition as advocates for children and immigrants by creating music videos and other digital content and sharing their work across platforms as @9thEvermore. He encourages his students to take the lead as creators in his classroom, coaching them as they craft their content and discover the power of their own voices.

John is the 2021 Utah Teacher of the Year and National Teacher of the Year Finalist. In 2023, he was recognized as one of Utah's *Most Valuable Educators* by Instructure and received a *K–12 Hero Award* from eSchool News. He is a National Board Certified Teacher and an adjunct professor in the Graduate School of Education at Westminster University. Beyond the classroom, John serves as the director of candidate recruitment for the Utah National Board Coalition, as well as the co-director of the Teacher Fellows, a nonpartisan nonprofit dedicated to developing the next generation of Utah teacher leaders.

As one of the United States' most renowned practicing teachers, John Arthur has delivered keynote addresses, participated on expert panels, and led professional learning for organizations, including the Smithsonian, SXSW EDU, National Science Teaching Association, Follett, and the National Network for State Teachers of the Year. John also serves on the board of directors for the National Board for Professional Teaching Standards, WestEd, REL West, and IncludEd United.

John received a bachelor's degree in English from the University of Utah, as well as master's degrees in both teaching and K–6 special education from Westminster University. He is currently pursuing his doctorate in educational policy, leadership, and management at Walden University.

To learn more about John Arthur's work, visit www.9thevermore.com or follow @9thEvermore on X, formerly known as Twitter.

To book John Arthur for professional development, contact pd@SolutionTree.com

# PREFACE

**ON WEDNESDAY, APRIL 16, 2014,** a ferry boat sank off the coast of South Korea. As the MV *Sewol* slowly listed on its side, passengers were told over the intercom to stay in their rooms; the captain and his crew then jumped into the sea and were immediately rescued. Recognizing that the *Sewol* was sinking, 158 passengers disregarded the announcement, left their rooms, and swam to safety. Tragically, 306 passengers, including 250 students from Danwon High School, did as they were told, remained in their rooms, and perished.

Twelve hours later, in Salt Lake City, Utah, I was driving to work early so I'd be the first in line at our school's one good copy machine. I was a first-year teacher, and my students had started end-of-year testing—testing my patience, my resolve, and which rules I was still willing to enforce. I turned on my radio, and that's when I heard the news about the students from Danwon High School.

Later, I told my fifth graders what I'd heard on the news; they could tell I was upset, but they didn't understand why.

"Did you know them?"

*No, I didn't know them—not all Koreans know each other.*

"So, are you mad because it's sad?"

*Yes, I'm mad because it's sad. It's so sad that 250 kids are dead because none of them said, "Hey, this boat is clearly sinking; let's get off the boat!" How did the students on that boat make it all the way to high school without learning how to think or speak for themselves? I mean, you wouldn't have stayed in your rooms, would you?*

As soon as the question entered my thoughts, I knew the answer was *yes*—my students would have done exactly as they were told, stayed in their rooms, and drowned, too.

At the time, it felt like I had failed my students. Sure, I'd taught them to think critically, but I never invited them to critique *my* thinking. I gave them permission to do this or that from time to time, but I never *empowered* them to make their own choices in a meaningful way.

That's when everything changed. For the rest of the year, I made empowerment the objective of every lesson. I invited my students to question every decision I made. When they asked me if they could use the restroom, I said things like, "Don't ask me for something you've got to have—tell me what you need, and then make it happen." This was clearly a drastic course correction from a flailing first-year teacher. Still, my students were loving it, and I felt like I was *finally* fulfilling the promises I'd made to myself when I entered teaching six months earlier.

One day, I asked my students, "If you could create anything together as an end-of-year project, what would it be?" A few of them suggested we make a music video, so I asked what they wanted to make a music video about.

One boy shouted, "Story problems!" My other students cheered, and I thought, *Oh my gosh, you are such nerds! But this is their project. Look how engaged they are. They're excited; this is good!*

"OK, story problems. Great, whose song do you want to cover?"

"One Direction!"

*Nooooooo!*

In that first music video, *The Story of Our Lives*, my students shared their favorite strategies for tackling story problems, including replacing the names with their own—that way, the stories were about them and the decisions they were making in their own lives. They sang in one voice:

*The story of our lives, we've taken control*
*We're the masters of our fates*
*Captains of our souls*
*Raise 'em high!*
*The story of our lives*

Sure, they lifted a couple of lines from William Ernest Henley's "Invictus," but I think their song would have made him proud.

 Don't take my word for how much my students enjoyed this song; scan the QR code and decide for yourself.

That was our first digital project—written, recorded, edited, and published using digital technology about a student-selected topic. Since then, my students have gained national recognition as champions for themselves, their families, and their communities thanks to the videos and other digital content they create and share across online platforms as @9thEvermore. They have appeared on television and radio interviews, their work has been featured on local programs like *PBS Utah* and *City Cast Salt Lake*, and they have presented at education conferences for administrators and teachers who are also committed to empowering their students' voices. Now, we are excited to open this window into our classroom and share our projects and practices with you!

# INTRODUCTION

> "Give the pupils something to do, not something to learn; and the doing is of such a nature as to demand thinking; learning naturally results."
>
> —John Dewey

**ASK ANY STUDENT WHAT** they want to be when they grow up, and many will say influencer, YouTuber, or content creator. Even if they say doctor, they really mean a doctor who makes TikToks. They will spend hours recording and rerecording the same video because they are intrinsically driven to create content for others to consume, which is perfect for us because that's what we ask of them every day—tell us about this, write about that, create a model of _____.

Instead of seeing our students as *kids in class*, what if we reframe them as *creators at work*? Why don't we leverage our students' talents to create original content for the concepts we're teaching, channeling their intrinsic drive into better versions of the assignments we already ask them to complete?

This book is my attempt at answering these questions—one teacher's do-it-yourself manual for creating digital projects in the classroom. This how-to guide is meant for upper-elementary and secondary classrooms and is designed to help teachers support their students in writing blog posts, preparing presentations, recording podcasts, and producing short films. It includes all the project descriptions, rubrics, reproducibles, and other documents I've created as scaffolds for my own students' creative work. However, don't picture me or my students as you read this book—picture *your* students (old or young) in *your* classroom (large or small) using whatever digital tools *you* have at hand.

These projects and practices can be adapted across grade levels and content areas because each is simply an engaging alternative to our current projects and practices. All of us rely on some combination of tests, quizzes, and assignments to assess our students' proficiency levels. However, by tossing aside even one tired assignment or assessment and replacing it with a digital project, the students' levels of satisfaction, motivation, and personal pride increase exponentially. It's a fantastic trade-off—think Indiana Jones in the cave, deftly swapping one weighted object for another, but instead we're tossing out the old bag of sand and replacing it with treasure.

Throughout this introduction, you'll learn about the benefits of digital projects, how to empower student voices, and how to engage parents and school leaders in these stimulating learning experiences. I'll then explain how you can get the most out of this book.

## The Benefits of Digital Projects

When sharing my students' work in keynotes and conferences around the United States, there are always teachers or administrators needing to see the research proving digital projects are effective evidence-based practices before bringing these projects back to their schools. The efficacy of these projects and practices rests in the same body of research built to support project-based learning; personalized, competency-based learning; and multimodal learning. Let's take a closer look at each of these.

### *Project-Based Learning*

*The Story of Our Lives*, described in the preface (page 2), was my first foray into project-based learning. While project-based learning doesn't have one exact definition, it typically includes identifying a project or problem that students work on individually or with peers, engaging in sustained inquiry, getting feedback and critique that supports revision, sharing the work with a wider audience, and then reflecting on the learning that happened across the whole process (Hough, 2022). With ideas dating back to the Progressive Era (approximately 1890–1920), project-based learning isn't new; however, its student-centered learning approach syncs well with a digital project's natural reliance on collaboration, critical thinking, communication, and technological integration (Hough, 2022).

The key to successfully implementing project-based learning is staying consistently engaged with students as they work on their projects. At the beginning of every project, I provide my students with an overview of the work they'll be doing, a rubric so they know what success looks like, and a planning page to help them get there. After that, I spend my time facilitating through feedback—circulating from one student or group to another—talking through their work depending on where they are in their creative process. For students to be successful in project-based learning, feedback in a high-trust environment must be thoroughly integrated into the learning cycle (Visible Learning, 2017). This feedback cycle helps students recognize that they have ownership over their work—I am present, but they're in charge. This student mindset best supports each project's underlying learning objectives because learning accelerates when the student, not the teacher, is taught to be in control of learning (Visible Learning, 2017). It would be lovely if we, as teachers, could present a digital project and send our students on their merry way while we catch up on emails. Unfortunately, the students would get frustrated, their projects would fail, and we would cheat ourselves of the joy of creating with students.

### *Personalized, Competency-Based Learning*

I first learned about competency-based learning from Sal Khan's (2015) TED Talk, "Let's Teach for Mastery, Not Test Scores." I was struck by the silliness of a system that advances students from one instruction unit to the next when compared with a house—"Would you choose to build a house on top of an unfinished foundation?" (Khan, 2015). I asked myself, "Why am I trying so hard to move all my students at the same pace through increasingly complicated mathematics and science concepts when their test scores show widening gaps in their individual levels of understanding?" Students should advance upon demonstrated mastery and receive timely, differentiated support based on their individual learning needs. These are the core tenets of the working definition of competency-based education developed in 2011 at the National Summit for K–12 Competency-Based Education (Sturgis, Patrick, & Pittenger, 2011). That definition was updated in 2019 to emphasize the importance of empowering students daily to make important decisions about their learning experiences, how they will create and apply knowledge, and how they will demonstrate learning (Levine & Patrick, 2019). Digital projects are the best means I have found to both empower students and implement competency-based learning in my classroom.

My home state of Utah has gone all-in on personalized, competency-based learning. In 2021, our legislature even codified personalized, competency-based learning in state statute, legally establishing it as a system of learning in which "Students are empowered daily to make important decisions about the students' learning experiences, how the students will create and apply knowledge, and how students will demonstrate the students' learning" (Utah State Legislature, 2021). This focus on student choice, voice, and agency—increasingly embraced by education stakeholders and now cemented in our state code—is the foundation on which digital projects stand as an innovative best practice. Our students must use their agency to progress toward academic proficiency by applying their knowledge, essential skills, and disposition toward meaningful and personally rewarding work. Few things are more personally rewarding for students than creating content around the topics they care about (Dickson, 2023).

## Multimodal Learning

Traditionally, teachers have favored text-based learning as the primary instruction approach—think textbooks, packets, worksheets, and so on. However, we are experiencing a proliferation of information in a variety of modes: gestures, visuals, haptics, auditory productions, and multimedia (Bouchey, Castek, & Thygeson, 2021). Multimodal learning can be defined as "learning environments that allow instructional elements to be presented in more than one sensory mode (visual, aural, written)" (Sankey, Birch, & Gardiner, 2010). Increased access to technological tools has further led to more modes for presenting, representing, and responding to information than ever before—that's why it's so important for us to provide multimodal learning environments and assignments that allow learners to receive and transmit information in various ways.

Bringing digital projects into your classroom provides students with dynamic opportunities to create using whatever sensory mode helps them best connect to the concepts you're teaching. Studies indicate that in comparison to traditional text-based, teacher-centered instructional approaches, multimodal and mastery learning approaches yield better student retention, more effective knowledge transfer, and greater student interest and positive attitudes because they are given wider opportunities to demonstrate content mastery (Montebello et al., 2019). Sure, these projects take time and effort. But when it comes to internalizing complex concepts, these projects are worth the investment because "the pedagogical and cognitive benefits of shifting meaning representation across a range of integrated modalities" greatly enrich student understanding (Montebello et al. 2019).

In previous years, a lack of suitable technology could have easily prevented many teachers from integrating digital projects into their lesson plans. However, while digital divides remain—particularly when it comes to at-home internet access—the switch to remote learning during the COVID-19 pandemic accelerated the trend toward greater access to computers, software, and other technologies in schools (Huebner & Burstein, 2023). When the world fell apart, laptops were our life vests, and a sea of endless software kept us afloat. Now, most teachers have the necessary technology and tools to implement project-based learning; personalized, competency-based learning; and multimodal learning, putting our students to work as content creators in our classrooms and empowering their voices in the process.

## Empowering Student Voices

After my third year of teaching, I moved up to sixth grade along with my fifth-grade class, and eventually, the stressors of new standards and a baby at home got the better of me. I started relying on super basic, teacher-led instruction and tired assignments to survive. Each day, my students worked packets, essays, and one-page worksheets in forty-five-minute blocks. Then, something interesting happened to the students I'd been with for over a year: they became quiet. Real quiet. They stopped talking in class, and my room was silent for long stretches each day. It was *amazing*, but I knew something was wrong. I asked one of my most outspoken students why she was suddenly so quiet. She said, "It doesn't feel like you want to hear what we have to say anymore."

Well, that shattered my teacher's heart. My students, who had felt so seen and heard by me just a year before, now felt unseen and powerless. I went home knowing I had months of mending and hard work ahead, but I knew I first had to survey the damage. So, I created this empowered student voices questionnaire (figure I.1) and asked my students to give my teaching practices an honest score.

I still administer this questionnaire once every quarter as a temperature check in my classroom; the less empowered my students feel, the more time I dedicate to content creation and digital projects. Like most teachers, I tend to do well on questions one and two—my students generally feel heard and have opportunities to share in class. My scores on questions three, four, and five go up and down depending on the time of year: in the early months, my students are learning our classroom structures and working through the 101 sections of this book, so more of our work together is teacher driven. Then, gradually, they take greater ownership of their learning and determine for themselves what topics they want to pursue and which projects to complete.

No score determines whether you've passed or failed as a teacher in empowering your students' voices; decide for yourself what a "winning" score would be and celebrate all progress in that direction. By the end of the year, my average is usually around a seven out of ten, which I think is pretty great. This tool can be very useful for gauging how empowered the adults in the room feel, too. If you're a coach or administrator, consider replacing *teacher* in figure I.2 (page 8) with your job title and *class* with your setting, and administer this questionnaire with the faculty or other personnel you lead. Remember, you can't give what you don't have—only empowered teachers can empower students.

## Engaging Parents and School Leaders

The first time I asked a parent if I could put their child on YouTube, I was sure they'd say *no*. Imagine my surprise when every parent I asked said *yes* and insisted I send them the link as soon as it was posted so they could share it with their friends! Even my principal was excited to share our students' work with her network. At first, I was confused, but seeing the same look in each

**Directions:** Please answer the following questions.

Name: _____   Score: _____ /10

2 = Strongly Agree, 1 = Agree, 0 = Neutral/Not Applicable,
−1 = Disagree, −2 = Strongly Disagree

| Question | Strongly Agree | Agree | Neutral | Disagree | Strongly Disagree |
|---|---|---|---|---|---|
| 1. My teacher wants to hear what I have to say. | | | | | |
| 2. I have frequent opportunities to share my perspectives in class. | | | | | |
| 3. I make choices about what I learn and how I demonstrate my learning. | | | | | |
| 4. I am proud of the work I create here and want to share it with others. | | | | | |
| 5. The work I create in class can change the way other people experience the world. | | | | | |

Comments:

**FIGURE I.1:** *Empowered student voices questionnaire.*

*Visit* **go.SolutionTree.com/technology** *for a free reproducible version of this figure.*

> 9th Evermore Media Release Form
>
> Dear Parents and Guardians,
>
> This year, your student will create incredible digital content for our class, including blog posts, short films, music videos, and podcasts! Past students have received national recognition and inspired countless children and teachers throughout our state with the content they've produced for our class's website and YouTube channel, 9thEvermore: http://www.youtube.com/c/9thEvermore
>
> With this release form, I am requesting permission for your student to participate in sharing the work they produce in our class. This includes reproducing and sharing all writing and digital media they create for these projects with our online community, including other teachers interested in recreating this powerful work in their own classrooms and schools. Your child's safety and privacy are my top concerns, and as such, your child's name or other information will not appear in any materials or media.
>
> Student: _____   Parent or Guardian: _____
>
> Parent or Guardian Signature: _____   Date: _____

**FIGURE I.2:** *Example media release form.*

parent's eyes, I realized what was driving their decision to allow their child to appear on the internet: pride. When my students made that music video about story problems, their parents wanted everyone in the world to see this incredible thing their children made in school.

You will need to secure two critical things before you can move forward in this work: (1) administrator approval and (2) parental permission. School leaders already must approve our content and curriculum. So, if you can clearly connect your students' digital creations to grade-level standards, no official approval or additional forms are typically required for your students' projects. However, before a project can be published online—even a written project like a blog post—you need to get a media release form signed by a parent or guardian. You can create your own media release form or use the form generated by your school or district's communications department. For comparison, figure I.2 is the media release form I send home on the first day of school each year, and figure I.3 is the form the Utah State Board of Education distributes before students appear in media or marketing materials.

Especially in areas with a tenuous political and social climate, use the form that will make you and your students' parents feel the safest and most secure when posting your students' creative content online.

## MEDIA RELEASE FORM

*Release of Rights for Photography and Multimedia Production*
*Reproduction and Commercial Display and Distribution*
*Use of Name and Written Quotes in Media and Publications*
*Original Producer/Owner*
*Utah State Board of Education*

I hereby grant permission to the Utah State Board of Education to use my photo and name in any media, advocacy, or marketing efforts to help promote the importance of Utah State Board of Education.

For good and valuable consideration, the receipt of which is hereby acknowledged, I hereby consent to the reproduction and/or authorization by the Utah State Board of Education to reproduce and use said photographs, recordings and/or digital media for use in all domestic foreign markets singularly or in conjunction with other photographs and digital media for advertising, publicity, commercial, or other business purposes. I understand that the term "photograph" as used herein encompasses still photographs, motion picture footage, and digital images of all kinds, and that the term "recordings" includes analog or digital recordings and reproductions.

Further, I understand that others, with or without the consent of the Utah State Board of Education, may use and/or reproduce such photographs and recording.

I hereby release the Utah State Board of Education, and any of its associates or affiliate companies, their directors, officers, agents, faculty, staff, students, and customers and any and all appointed advertising agencies, their directors, officers, agents, and employees from all claims of every kind on account of such use or reproduction.

Name: _____    Phone number: _____
           *Please print*

Email: _____    School: _____

Signature of student: _____    Date: _____

Signature of parent or guardian: _____    Date: _____
*(Required if student is under 18 years of age)*

*Source: Utah State Board of Education, n.d.*
**FIGURE I.3:** *Utah State Board of Education media release form.*

## How to Use This Book

This book includes six digital projects—one project per chapter, spread across two parts—depending on the type of content you want your students to create. Each part begins with a chapter to serve as a 101 crash course, equipping you with the knowledge and skills needed to guide students to successfully complete their projects. The subsequent chapters in each part detail different digital projects you can empower students with. The breakdown of each part is as follows.

- **Part I:** Digital voices 101 (chapter 1), blog posts (chapter 2), presentations (chapter 3), and podcasts (chapter 4)
- **Part II:** Digital videos 101 (chapter 5), documentary short films (chapter 6), narrative short films (chapter 7), and music videos (chapter 8)

Each chapter will provide research on the pedagogical benefits of each project type, recommendations regarding media literacy and online research, materials lists, tech tools and tips, and best practices for amplifying your students' voices. You will also find QR codes throughout the book that link to videos created by my students, which you can use as models in your instruction.

Each project includes a vignette of my creators at work, an introduction to the project itself, a rubric, a student planning page, links to models and exemplars, graphic organizers, and other instructional materials. I have also added practical advice and personal anecdotes from my classroom so you have a sense of what each project implementation might look and sound like in real life.

You can treat this collection of lesson plans like a cookbook—maybe you start with the first project and work your way through, or perhaps you jump from one project to another depending on your students' interests and tastes. Don't be surprised if the pages of your favorite reproducibles end up just as dog-eared as your family's favorite recipes. The more projects your students complete in class, the more versatile they will become as content creators, and the more likely they will be to discover the digital medium that best fits their interests. Finally, in this book's conclusion, I bring us back to the beating heart of this work—reframing our students as content creators, empowering their voices, and why both are so *necessary*.

PDF versions of all resources shared in this book can be found online on the Solution Tree website (visit **go.SolutionTree.com/technology**). Each resource can be printed as is, or you can modify it to meet your class's needs. The goal of this book is to elevate your students' work and share it with a broader audience, so please use these projects and resources in any way that makes them the most manageable and meaningful for you and your students.

# PART I
# DIGITAL VOICES

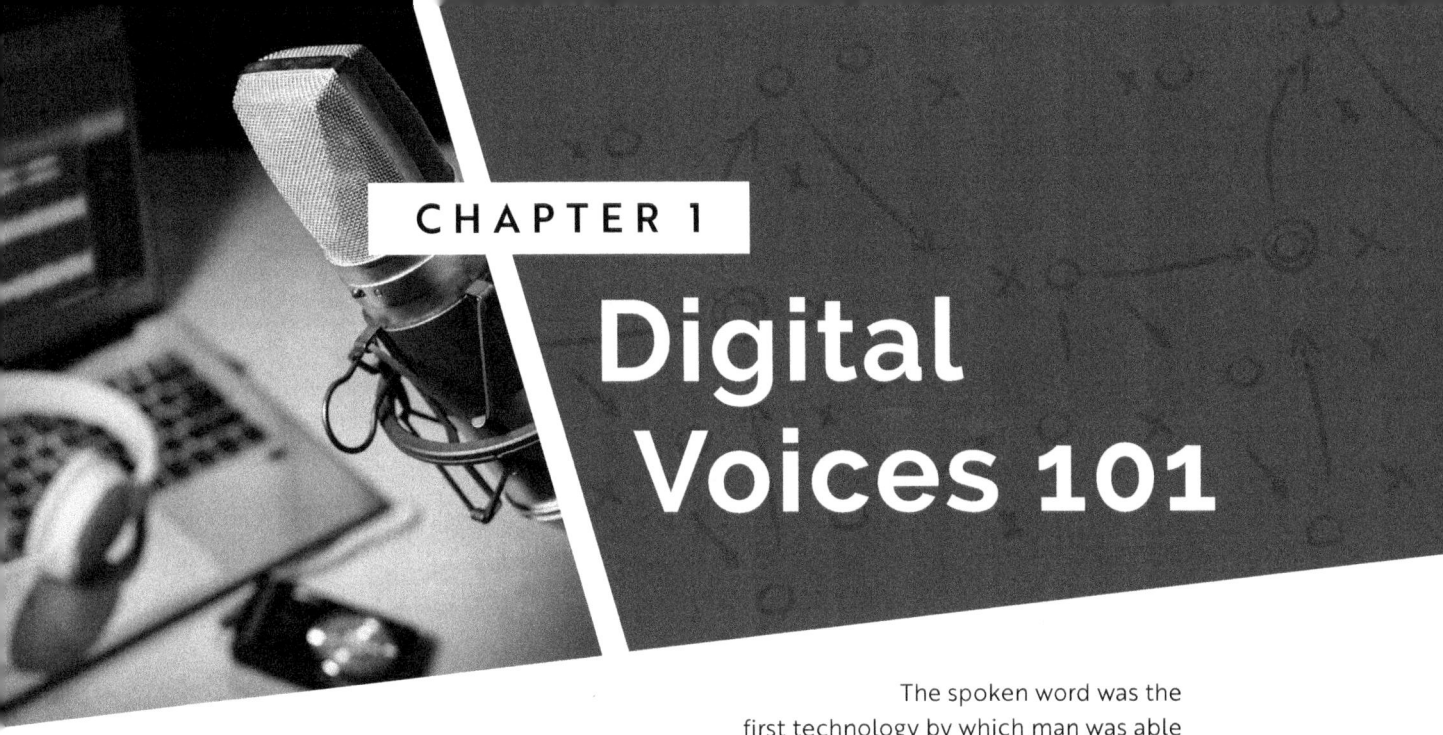

# CHAPTER 1

# Digital Voices 101

> The spoken word was the
> first technology by which man was able
> to let go of his environment in order to grasp it in a new way.
> Words are a kind of information retrieval that can range over the total
> environment and experience at high speed.
>
> —*Marshall McLuhan*

**EVERY STATE AND PROVINCE** sets academic standards for student learning, and every teacher is accountable for teaching those standards. In my first year of teaching, I was shown Utah's English language arts power standards—the knowledge and skills designated as most essential for students to master in a particular content area—by the instructional coach at my school. However, Utah has since adopted the Common Core State Standards (National Governors Association Center for Best Practices & Council of Chief State School Officers [NGA & CCSSO], 2010). In all our conversations together, I kept noticing that there was one English language arts standard the instructional coach kept skipping (one might even say *avoiding*):

> W.5.6: . . . use technology, including the Internet, to produce and publish writing as well as to interact and collaborate with others. (NGA & CCSSO, 2010)

When I read this standard aloud to my coach, she suddenly became anxious, stammering over her words like I'd stumbled on a dark family secret. "Oh, W.5.6 . . . Well, it's awfully hard to teach and isn't all that useful." This answer confused me for two reasons: (1) I've never used *it's hard to teach* as a reason *not* to teach, and (2) this coach was a prolific and well-known blogger! How can a standard not be useful if you use it all the time?

This is now my favorite standard. Teaching my students to use technology and the internet to produce and publish their writing as blog posts, presentations, podcasts, or videos excites me most as a classroom teacher. Note that Utah's English language arts standard W.5.6 mirrors the Common Core State Writing standards (NGA & CCSSO, 2010) for students throughout U.S. grades 4–12. More than likely, your state or province wants you to be teaching it, too.

The challenge lies in the *how*. We all know this is the work we need to be doing, but we don't always know quite how to do it. That's why I'm so excited to share these digital projects with you! In this chapter, you'll ease into that work by reviewing step-by-step instructions for transforming your traditional writing assignments and presentations into digital projects that the content creators in your classroom will love. You'll get some baseline knowledge about this part's chapter topics (blogging, presentations, and podcasts); review some best practices for online research, media literacy, and use of artificial intelligence (AI); and engage with some tools and tips for creating digital content in the classroom.

## Benefits of Blogging, Presentations, and Podcasts

Blogging, oral presentations, and podcasts are included together in this book because they are all variations on projects that teachers are familiar with and feel more comfortable executing in their own classrooms. There are similarities in the research supporting each as an effective instructional practice; however, I'm presenting them individually to highlight the unique benefits of all three projects.

### *Blogging*

In the *International Education Studies* article, "The Effectiveness of Using Online Blogging for Students' Group Writing," author Hashem A. Alsamadani (2018) finds that students who blog show noticeable improvement in several writing areas, such as content development, language mechanics, style, voice, and word choice. Interestingly, research also indicates that blogging benefits students in areas outside of writing, including digital literacy, personal expression, social and civic competencies, self-perceived motivation, and the ability to collaborate with others (Campillo-Ferrer, Miralles-Martinez, & Sanchez-Ibanez, 2021).

The improvement in students' collaborative skills is particularly interesting to me. Writing is typically considered a solitary endeavor—the author alone in their garret, silently struggling as life goes on without them. Case in point, I am literally sitting alone in my home office writing this chapter, watching my daughters have the time of their lives playing outside without me.

However, thanks to its interactivity and immediacy, blogging can be an incredibly collaborative activity for students, one in which they receive guidance, engagement, feedback, and support from friends in class, in virtual learning communities, and among worldwide internet users. (Kuo, Belland, & Kuo, 2017). Blogs can also be written by groups of students working together, which often helps improve students' writing skills more than working individually due to the constant interpretation, analysis, and feedback group members receive through discussions and debates (Alsamadani, 2018). Over time, creating digital content with others builds collaborative competencies that naturally translate into stronger social and civic skills in our youth, producing better students, citizens, and leaders in our communities.

In my experience, when students realize their work will be posted in places where anyone can see and read it, they take greater care with what they write and revise it to produce better work. This trend holds true for students of all ages writing blogs across different content areas. For example, a study of first-year university students writing a collaborative blog in an introductory cell biology course finds that the blog's public exposure provided students with a strong sense of competence, value (usefulness), and connection with their topics, leading them to work on the blog in an intrinsically motivated fashion (Kramer & Kusurkar, 2017). Also motivating for undergraduates is the opportunity to freely express their views on current issues and provoke a reaction from their readers (Halic, Lee, Paulus, & Spence, 2010). These outcomes may particularly interest secondary teachers who might see the same benefits for their students.

Greater student engagement, collaboration, self-motivation, skills, and purpose: What more could a teacher ask for?

## Presentations

Since 2000, a whole industry has sprung up around public speaking, allowing professional presenters to earn a living by informing, inspiring, and captivating audiences with their words. An article in the *Harvard Business Review* recommends beginning speakers charge $500–$10,000 for a talk, whereas well-known speakers, such as best-selling authors, can comfortably charge $20,000–$35,000 per talk (Clark, 2018). Use these facts on the financial incentives for mastering public speaking to impress that student who's always asking, "How much will I get paid for this?" Well, *I* won't pay you anything, but someday someone might.

For my fellow educators and administrators, there are several pedagogical advantages to incorporating recorded oral presentations into your course curriculum. These presentations:

- Reinforce students' research skills
- Challenge students to better organize information and articulate their learning
- Encourage students to explore their creativity
- Promote students' knowledge retention
- Develop at an early age the requisite skills elementary and secondary students will eventually need to succeed in higher education
- Enhance their postgraduation employability (Liao, Lewis, & Winiski, 2020)

The social component of presenting in front of peers also benefits both the presenter and their audience (Moody, 2016). Students are more motivated to get the explanations right when they are presenting in class, especially when they know they're being recorded and their presentation will be available to view online, like a TED Talk. This pays dividends in students' own understanding, while others in class learn from each presenter's mistakes or good modeling (Moody, 2016). Presentations are also a highly effective mode of assessment, both formative and summative, across age groups and content areas (Tsang, 2017). Best of all, when their presentation is recorded, students can self-assess their performance when they watch the playback.

In the introduction (page 3), I outlined how digital projects align with several pedagogical approaches, including multimodal learning. Again, as we experience the proliferation of information in a variety of modes, we must cultivate learning environments that deliver instruction through written, visual, and aural means. Presentations incorporate all these learning modes, efficiently addressing the various processing needs of a diverse audience (Manfre, 2021). Whether presentations are performed live or recorded for a future webinar, they allow audiences to experience the information in multiple ways, which increases the likelihood that they will retain and productively incorporate that information or message into their daily lives.

Finally, our teaching standards insist we create and deliver presentations. The College and Career Readiness (CCR) anchor standards for grades 6–12 include Speaking and Listening standards that support the creation of digital presentations in any secondary setting (NGA & CCSSO, 2010):

- **CCRA.SL.3:** Evaluate a speaker's point of view, reasoning, and use of evidence and rhetoric.

- **CCRA.SL.4:** Present information, findings, and supporting evidence such that listeners can follow the line of reasoning and the organization, development, and style are appropriate to the task, purpose, and audience.
- **CCRA.SL.5:** Make strategic use of digital media and visual displays of data to express information and enhance understanding of presentations.

Standards that mirror these are almost certainly found in your state, too. These standards affirm educators who know they're doing their best work when students are empowered to present original works to their peers, both in the room and online.

## Podcasts

This generation of students (and some of you reading right now) has never known a time when the internet and digital tools were not an integral part of their personal and scholastic life (McCarron & Yamanaka, 2022). In 2019, the total number of people ages 12 and older who had ever listened to a podcast passed 50 percent for the first time (Nelson, 2021). Podcasting has seen explosive year-over-year growth in popularity, and for the digital natives in our schools, creating podcasts is a fun and instructionally effective way of connecting classwork with one of their favorite forms of entertainment.

During the pandemic, assigning podcasts for students to listen to asynchronously became a go-to practice that allowed our students much-needed autonomy and flexibility. Considering the increased responsibilities many students had to take on, the ability to download an audio file and listen when they could engage more fully helped many students complete remote-learning coursework (McCarron & Yamanaka, 2022). Generation Z students especially enjoy learning at their own pace—a feature podcasts provide. The review aspect of podcasts—being able to slow down or rewind instruction as needed—is particularly helpful for multilingual learners and students with visual impairment or dyslexia (Woodward, 2022). Also, whereas visual materials allow the viewer to passively consume the content, audio material requires active listening and audiences willing to imagine the context of people, space, and place in a recording (Waldron, Covington, & Palmer, 2023).

Once students transition from simply listening to recorded files to creating their own podcasts, they become even more engaged and active in their learning. Students become active producers rather than passive consumers of knowledge as they formulate scripts, learn how to research as part of the production process, record their content, and edit their final products (Dversnes & Blikstad-Balas, 2023). The recording studio becomes the perfect setting for what the late, legendary Brazilian educator Paulo Freire (2017) calls a "space of reciprocity and dialogue" where problem-posing education creates a site of mutual engagement in the production of knowledge and "the practice of freedom" (p. 81).

In the context of podcast production, the mutual engagement Freire (2017) points to depends on our students engaging in dialogue with community members they interview and one another. The benefits of student dialogue include the development of reasoning skills, improved conversations about challenging academic concepts in core subjects like mathematics and science, and opportunities for students to recognize the importance of their own voices as they try out and modify their thoughts and build on others' ideas (Dversnes & Blikstad-Balas, 2023). When framed as a group assignment, podcast episode creation also requires students to practice relationship and negotiation skills, which are highly transferable to a variety of professional contexts (Hitchcock, Sage, Lynch, & Sage, 2021).

Finally, what I love most about podcasting in the classroom is the opportunity to promote marginalized voices that are not easily accessible in more traditional media formats (Hitchcock et al., 2021). Student-generated podcasts often shine a light on linguistic diversity in our schools and celebrate alternative ways of interpreting our own lived experiences. In addition to creating empathy and understanding, podcasts provide a pedagogical tool for students to learn how to listen to and hear the voices of people who may hold other views, who worship differently, or who have faced challenges that are very different from—or very similar to—their own (Waldron et al., 2023). Student podcasts can have the same transformative effect on a variety of adult audiences beyond the classroom, including community leaders and policymakers (Hitchcock et al., 2021). By creating podcasts that concisely capture the messages and stories they feel compelled to share, students can use these digital projects to advocate for themselves and expand the understanding of adults who make decisions that affect their everyday lives.

## Online Research, Media Literacy, and Artificial Intelligence

As we send our content creators forth into the digital landscape to gather information, play with tools, and publish their work, we must do so with an abundance of caution and a healthy respect for the inherent risks. In this section, we will cover resources and lessons related to online research, media literacy, and AI to prepare our students to safely navigate the vast sea of information available online.

### *Online Research*

For our work in the classroom, *online research* refers to the process students undertake to gather information, data, and multimedia resources from the internet for their digital projects. It involves using various digital tools, search engines, databases, and educational websites to access reliable and relevant information. Teaching our students to conduct online research equips them with the ability to organize information from multiple digital platforms, explore diverse perspectives, and synthesize information to develop original ideas about their chosen topics. This is an essential skill for students in the digital age, enabling them to navigate and leverage the vast resources available on the internet for success in and out of our classrooms.

I use three activities to teach my students the essentials of conducting online research: (1) ten facts about Cesar Chavez, (2) internet safety vocabulary search, and (3) copyright infringement or fair use? Each of these activities will be explained in more detail in the following sections, but first, it's important to know how to make web browser searches both safe and effective for students.

#### *Safe and Effective Online Search Tools*

The following websites are generally safe for student use in learning activities.

- **Google Scholar (https://scholar.google.com):** This search engine allows students to find scholarly literature across many disciplines and sources: articles, theses, books, abstracts, and court opinions from academic publishers, professional societies, online repositories, universities, and other websites. Google Scholar also ranks documents the way researchers do, weighing the full text of each document, where it was published, who wrote it, and how recently it has been cited in scholarly literature.

- **Sweet Search (www.sweetsearch.com):** This search engine is designed for students and only provides reliable and credible sources. It leverages Google to search only a safe list of websites that has been fully vetted and ranked by teachers and librarians, rather than relying on filters like other search engines do.
- **Kiddle (www.kiddle.co):** This search engine is similarly designed for students, especially elementary students. It offers safe web, image, and video search results that are vetted by editors and filtered to ensure that they are appropriate for children. Kiddle encyclopedia (Kpedia; https://kids.kiddle.co) is an online encyclopedia, available through the Kiddle search engine that lists over 700,000 articles. This is a great resource; however, Kpedia's articles are based on selected content and facts from Wikipedia that are rewritten for children, so students should cross-reference information drawn from this user-edited source to avoid including errors or misleading content in their own projects.

One of the lesser-known secrets of using search engines effectively is the variety of terms that students can use to modify their searches and narrow their results to the most useful resources possible. While these tricks work well on Google, other search engines with similar features might use different syntax or adhere to their own specific rules.

- **Boolean operators:** Use AND, OR, and NOT to combine or exclude specific terms in your search. For example, the search *climate change AND effects* retrieves results that include both terms, while *climate change NOT politics* returns results regarding climate change that exclude results related to politics.
- **Phrase searching:** Use quotation marks to search for an exact phrase. For example, searching for *"housing crisis"* will only retrieve results that contain the phrase in that specific order.
- **Wildcard searches:** Use an asterisk (*) as a placeholder for unknown words or to find word variations. For example, *teach\** retrieves results for *teach, teaching, teacher,* and so on.
- **Synonym searching:** Use the tilde (~) before a word to include synonyms and alternative endings in your search results. For example, searching for *~healthy recipes* will retrieve results for both *healthy recipes* and similar phrases like *nutritious meals* or *wholesome cooking.*
- **Site-specific searches:** Limit your search to a specific website or domain by using the *site:* operator. For example, *site:.edu* will only retrieve results from websites for U.S. educational and academic institutions.

### Activity: Ten Facts About Cesar Chavez

In this activity, students use tips found in the "Safe and Effective Online Search Tools" (page 17) to find ten facts about Cesar Chavez. Figure 1.1 contains a blank example of the activity, while figure 1.2 provides a version with correct student answers.

You should also discuss the importance of the following best practices as you introduce your students to these tools.

1. Cross-referencing information from multiple sources to verify the accuracy of answers
2. Paying attention to website domains (such as .edu, .gov, and .com) to assess the source's reliability and potential bias
3. Engaging in peer collaboration as a means of more quickly finding information, as well as an opportunity to discuss findings, share reliable sources, and exchange feedback

**Directions:** Use the Search Browsers for Students and Online Research Tips and Tricks to find the missing information in the following statements.

1. Cesar Chavez was born in _____, _____, in 19___.
2. Cesar Chavez had _____ siblings.
3. During the _____, the family lost their farm and moved to _____.
4. Cesar Chavez had to quit school in _____ grade to earn money for his family.
5. Cesar Chavez worked as a _____, which meant that when he finished harvesting one type of crop, he moved to another farm for more work.
6. Cesar Chavez served the United States by joining the _____ in 19___.
7. Cesar Chavez started two organizations to fight for better working conditions for farm workers:

    _____ in 1952.

    _____ in 1962.
8. Cesar Chavez used _____ protests, like strikes, boycotts, and marches, to achieve his goals.
9. Cesar Chavez called his movement "_____," which means The Cause.
10. Cesar Chavez was well known for _____ or going without food for a period of time. His longest _____ lasted _____ days.

**FIGURE 1.1:** *Activity—Ten facts about Cesar Chavez.*

Visit **go.SolutionTree.com/technology** *for a free reproducible version of this figure.*

---

Directions: Use the Search Browsers for Students and Online Research Tips and Tricks to find the missing information in the following statements.

1. Cesar Chavez was born in __Yuma__, __Arizona__, in 19_27_.
2. Cesar Chavez had __five__ siblings.
3. During the __Great Depression__, the family lost their farm and moved to __California__.
4. Cesar Chavez had to quit school in __eighth__ grade to earn money for his family.

**FIGURE 1.2:** *Activity—Ten facts about Cesar Chavez (answer key).*

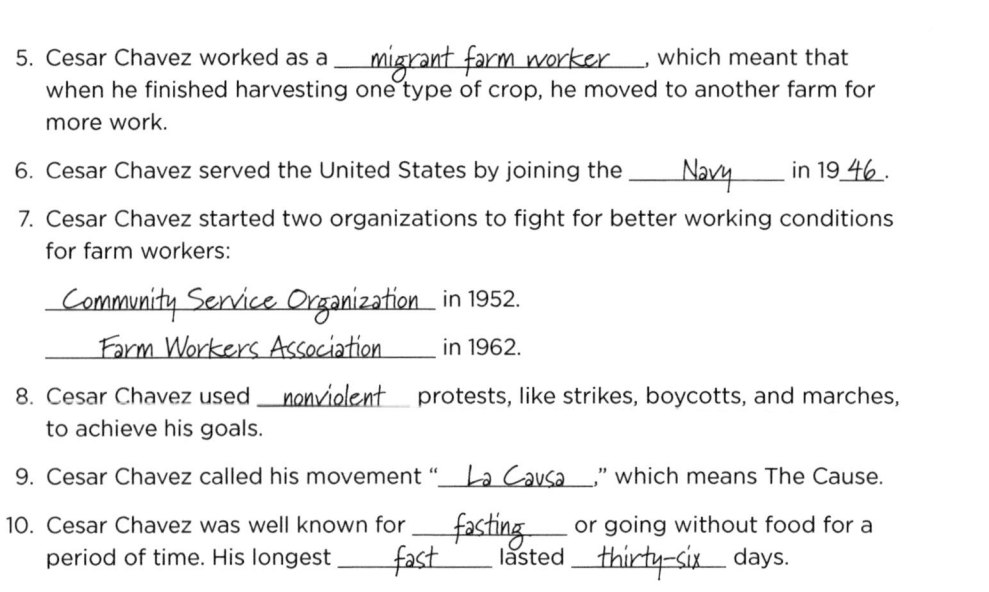

Visit **go.SolutionTree.com/technology** for a free reproducible version of this figure.

I chose Cesar Chavez as the subject for this activity because his work aligns with Utah's fifth-grade social studies standards, and he is an important historical figure for the families in my school community. You should adapt this lesson as needed to fit the age group, community, and content area you teach.

### Activity: Internet Safety Vocabulary Search

Students again use the appropriate browsers and search operators described in the "Safe and Effective Online Search Tools" section (page 17) to find the definitions for five key terms: (1) *personally identifiable information*, (2) *identity theft*, (3) *phishing scams*, (4) *strong passwords*, and (5) *cyberbullying*. Students must go online to find a comprehensive definition for each key term, including a link to their online source, and provide at least one real-world example per term. Figure 1.3 shows an example of a completed version of this vocabulary search. While my sixth-grade students have successfully completed this assignment independently year after year, I would go through this activity as a whole group with younger students.

### Activity: Copyright Infringement or Fair Use?

In this activity, students explore the legal and ethical aspects of using copyrighted materials. Working with copyrighted materials can be complicated, but if you and your students follow the general small amounts for educational purposes principle, you should have little trouble incorporating portions of copyrighted materials into your digital projects.

As a teacher, it's important for you to have a basic understanding of copyright and fair use so you can facilitate a class discussion on the importance of protecting content creators' rights and avoiding plagiarism. For this discussion, it's important to know and be able to convey to students the following foundational knowledge.

| Key Vocabulary | Definition and Source | Example |
|---|---|---|
| **Personally identifiable information** | Personally identifiable information directly identifies an individual (for example, name, address, social security number or other identifying number or code, telephone number, email address, and so on), indirectly identifies an individual (for example, a combination of gender, race, birth date, geographic indicator, and other descriptors), or permits the physical or online contacting of a specific individual. (U.S. Department of Labor, 2024) | 8**-***-**** |
| **Identity theft** | Identity theft is a crime in which someone wrongfully obtains and uses another person's personal data in some way that involves fraud or deception, typically for economic gain. (Department of Justice, 2023) | An ID thief uses your credit card number to buy a laptop on Amazon |
| **Phishing scams** | Phishing scams are a type of online scam that targets consumers by sending them an email that appears to be from a well-known source—an internet service provider, a bank, or a mortgage company, for example. It asks the consumer to provide personal identifying information. Then, a scammer uses the information to open new accounts or invade the consumer's existing accounts. Avoid phishing scams by not responding to emails or pop-up messages that ask for personal or financial information. (Federal Trade Commission, 2024) | An email that says you'll receive a big tax refund immediately if you just click on the link and input your personal identifiable information |
| **Strong passwords** | Strong passwords are hard to determine both by humans and by the computer. Two things make a password stronger: (1) a larger number of characters and (2) mixing numeric digits, upper- and lower-case letters, and special characters ($, #, and so on). Never use personal information in your password, and don't use the same password for multiple accounts. (GCFGlobal, 2024) | m#P52s@ap$V |
| **Cyberbullying** | Cyberbullying is bullying that takes place over digital devices like cell phones, computers, and tablets. Cyberbullying can occur through SMS, text, and apps, or online in social media, forums, or gaming where people can view, participate in, or share content. Cyberbullying includes sending, posting, or sharing negative, harmful, false, or mean content about someone else. Some cyberbullying crosses the line into unlawful or criminal behavior. (StopBullying.gov, 2021) | A classmate constantly instant messaging mean and hurtful comments to another |

**FIGURE 1.3:** *Internet safety vocabulary search example answers.*
*Visit **go.SolutionTree.com/technology** for a free reproducible version of this figure.*

Copyrights automatically protect all original, creative work in a fixed form the moment it is created. Works created after January 1, 1978, are covered by copyright for a term equaling the author's life plus seventy years following their death. For works created before 1978, copyright duration varies but typically lasts for fifty years before works enter the public domain (Lagola, 2021). Copyright does not apply to facts, public information, print maps, or government documents or pictures, so resources from organizations like NASA, the Smithsonian, and the National Archives can be used without permission (Lagola, 2021).

The fair use doctrine allows teachers and students to use copyrighted materials in educational settings under the following four conditions (U.S. Copyright Office, 2023).

1. **Purpose and character of the use:** Nonprofit educational and noncommercial uses are more likely to be found fair in court. Additionally, *transformative* uses that add something new, with a further purpose or different character from the original work, are more likely to be considered fair.

2. **Nature of the copyrighted work:** Using a more creative or imaginative work (such as a novel, movie, or song) is less likely to support a fair use claim than using a factual work (such as a technical article or news item). In addition, using an unpublished work is less likely to be considered fair.

3. **Amount and substantiality of the portion related to the copyrighted work as a whole:** If the use includes a large portion of the copyrighted work, fair use is less likely to be found; if the use employs only a small amount of copyrighted material, fair use is more likely.

4. **Effect on the potential market for or value of the copyrighted work:** Here, courts review whether and to what extent the unlicensed use harms the existing or future market for the copyright owner's original work. Courts consider whether the use is hurting the current market for the original work (for example, by displacing sales of the original) or whether the use could cause substantial harm if it becomes widespread.

Obviously, you will have to tailor your explanations of fair use to fit your students' developmental level. After facilitating this overview with students, have them complete the worksheet shown in figure 1.4 in pairs or small groups.

### Media Literacy

On its website, the National Association for Media Literacy Education (NAMLE, 2024) describes *media literacy* as "the ability to access, analyze, evaluate, create, and act using all forms of communication." This dynamic set of skills builds on traditional literacy by teaching students to critically examine stories and information found online or in print to determine their accuracy and credibility. With the proliferation of online news sources, social media, and deceptive advertisements, it is essential for students to become discerning consumers of information, capable of differentiating between reliable sources and those that are fake or biased. Teaching media literacy fosters empathy and digital citizenship in our youth, encouraging them to lead as positive contributors in their online and real-world communities.

Thankfully, there are wonderful resources to help teachers deliver simple, high-quality lessons that guide students around the pitfalls of misinformation and propaganda. I use three free

**Directions:** Determine whether the use of materials in each scenario constitutes copyright infringement or fair use. In each scenario, consider the purpose and character of the use, nature of the copyrighted work, the amount used, and the effect on the potential market for the original work while making your determinations.

| Scenarios | Copyright Infringement or Fair Use | Explanation |
|---|---|---|
| **Scenario 1:** Gabriela is a student working on a school project. She finds an interesting article online and copies and pastes the entire text into her project without giving any credit to the original author. Is this copyright infringement or fair use? | | |
| **Scenario 2:** Peter is a musician and wants to post covers of popular songs on his YouTube channel. He records himself singing and playing the guitar to recreate these songs. Is this copyright infringement or fair use? | | |
| **Scenario 3:** Sarah is a high school teacher preparing materials for her class. She copies an entire chapter from a textbook and distributes it to her students without permission from the publisher. Is this copyright infringement or fair use? | | |
| **Scenario 4:** Marcus is writing a research paper and needs to include a few quotes from a book he found in the library. He properly cites the author and the source. Is this copyright infringement or fair use? | | |
| **Scenario 5:** Alex is an artist who finds a photograph online that he wants to use as a reference for his painting. He copies the photograph exactly and sells his painting without obtaining permission from the original photographer. Is this copyright infringement or fair use? | | |

***FIGURE 1.4:*** *Copyright infringement or fair use?*

| | | |
|---|---|---|
| **Scenario 6:**<br>Maya is a documentary filmmaker and wants to include clips from famous movies to provide historical context in her film. She plans to use short segments and properly credit the movies used in her film. Is this copyright infringement or fair use? | | |
| **Scenario 7:**<br>Juan is a student who loves photography. He takes a photo of a famous landmark from the internet and edits it using photo editing software. He shares the edited photo on social media without any attribution or permission from the original photographer. Is this copyright infringement or fair use? | | |
| **Scenario 8:**<br>Emma is a student creating a presentation for class. She includes images from a website that are labeled for noncommercial use only. She uses them in her school project without seeking permission. Is this copyright infringement or fair use? | | |

*Visit **go.SolutionTree.com/technology** for a free reproducible version of this figure.*

resources to teach media literacy in my classroom. With each resource, you will find a sequence of lesson plans that build on each other, along with worksheets, videos, graphic organizers, and recommendations for engaging students in collaborative discussions.

1. **Meet the Media Monsters (from NAMLE; https://tinyurl.com/59ry6ea5):**
   This resource may have been designed for students in grades 3–5, but I have had great success using these three lessons with my sixth-grade students. I start my media literacy unit with this resource because it teaches students to identify and reflect on their own behaviors and media practices. NAMLE's goal is to help students recognize how they engage with media, think critically about the media messages around them, and overcome their own *media monster* behavior.

2. **Media Literacy 101 (from Media Smarts; https://mediasmarts.ca/media-literacy-101):**
   This resource offers six short videos (each roughly one-and-a-half minutes long) that introduce students to the key concepts of media literacy and provide an effective foundation for examining mass media and popular culture. Each video is accompanied by a lesson plan that provides educators with everything they need—learning outcomes, materials, procedures, and optional extension tasks—to help students internalize the video's main idea and apply what they've learned with their peers.

3. **News and Media Literacy 101 (Common Sense Education; www.commonsense.org /education/articles/news-media-literacy-101):** I've listed this resource third because

that's how I structure my instructional sequence; however, this is the tool I rely on most in teaching media literacy to my students. In addition to videos and worksheets, Common Sense's lessons are drawn from its own K–12 Digital Citizenship Curriculum and include slide decks with everything needed to teach these lessons already embedded, key vocabulary with definitions, and prompts to spark classroom debates. My favorite lesson is "Hoaxes and Fakes," which teaches students not to be duped by fake viral videos by going elsewhere online to check credibility and find corroboration for what they've just seen.

### *Artificial Intelligence*

Much has already been said about the groundbreaking effect of generative AI (often referred to as *large language models*) on the education landscape. By the time you're reading this, all those insights will already be dated, so I'll keep this section brief. I personally align with those who think of AI as *assistive intelligence*—technology that can help our students access more digital tools in less time, support their research endeavors, and provide meaningful feedback as they pursue academic excellence. As for teachers, in the words of ChatGPT-4, "While AI can be a powerful tool in education, it is best seen as a supplement to human teachers, not a replacement" (OpenAI, 2023). This is correct. Instead, think of large language models and other AI models as complements and amplifiers of expertise.

The digital projects in this book are designed to empower student voices as they create original works—it's up to you to decide what role, if any, generative AI will play in that process. At the end of the day, I recommend focusing your interest primarily on what students create, not what the technology can do. Generative AI can't stand up in front of a room full of peers and deliver an oral presentation. As for its writing, AI is a predictive tool, and our students' voices—whether written or recorded—are gloriously unpredictable. If anything, the scorching growth of generative AI underscores the necessity of reframing students in class as creators at work. Since generative AI can do everything else for us, I say we double down on human creativity and make mining our students' inherent brilliance the whole point of everything we do in school.

- - -

## Digital Tools and Technology Tips

It's not enough to say that a student just needs a computer to write a blog post, create a presentation, or record a podcast. A computer is like a suitcase—you must pack it for the journey ahead. First, for the digital projects here in part I, make sure the suitcases themselves are in good working order: the cameras are clean, microphones sound good, and keyboards have every key accounted for. Maybe you'll want to pack an external microphone, camera, or webcam for improved audio and video recording—wonderful to have, but not a must. Do you have all the software you'll need? I'm guessing you're all set with your word processor and presentation software, but what about a video conferencing tool like Webex or Zoom or a screen recorder like Screencastify or Loom?

Figure 1.5 (page 26) lists all the digital resources students will need to complete the projects in part I, along with the tools I've seen and encouraged my students to use in our classroom.

I teach in a district that uses Windows PCs and Microsoft Office; wherever you teach, use the tools your school provides and those your creators are most comfortable with. The first five digital tools listed in figure 1.5 are necessities for this section's projects, and the other five are nice to haves that can enhance the quality and appeal of your students' work.

| Digital Tool Category | Examples Tools for This Category |
|---|---|
| **Essential Tools** ||
| Computer with camera and microphone | Dell Windows Laptop |
| Word processor | Microsoft Word |
| Presentation software | PowerPoint, Canva |
| Audio recording software | Zoom, Adobe Audition, Audacity, GarageBand |
| Audio editing software | Adobe Audition, Adobe Enhance, Adobe Express, Canva |
| **Nice-to-Have Tools** ||
| External microphone | Yeti microphone |
| External camera or webcam | iPhone, Logitech webcam, Canon DSLR camera |
| Video conferencing tool or screen recorder | Zoom, Loom |
| Video editing software | Adobe Express, iMovie, Canva |
| Learning management system or podcast hosting platform | Canvas, Simple |

**FIGURE 1.5:** *Digital tools list.*

Regardless of which tools you adopt in your classroom, know that the world of word processors, audio editors, and presentation platforms available for student use is so vast and evolves so quickly that providing any sort of tutorial on a specific tool would be a waste of your time. However, the following five tips for creating digital content in the classroom are drawn from my students' experiences and are useful to implement across tools and platforms.

### *Create a Digital Project Folder*

Before you begin any digital project, create a digital folder for that project housed on a shared drive (such as Google Drive, Microsoft OneDrive, or Microsoft Teams) that you and your students can all access. Within that digital folder, create individual folders for each content creator containing the rubric, planning page, drafting templates, and so on, for that project. This way, all work for a particular project is kept nicely in the same digital location, and you won't have to waste time wondering where on their computers your students are saving their stuff.

### *Find Your Mavens*

Students enter your room with varying mastery levels of technology and specific tools. One of their former teachers may have been a big fan of Prezi for creating slide presentations, while another might have taught students how to create in PowerPoint. During the first few weeks of school, assign short digital projects that help you identify those students that I like to call my mavens. A *maven* is a specialist or expert in a specific area. In your digital workshop, your mavens are the creators you can call on when you can't figure out how to make something work. They're the students whose past experiences with a platform or tool make it appear that they just get it, and these mavens are not hard to find. Empower them to support their peers who are acquainting themselves with unfamiliar technologies, and honor students' expertise by entrusting them with leadership opportunities throughout the creative process. Here are three projects I have my students complete in the first two weeks of school to help me find my mavens.

1. **Identity infographic:** Students select a Canva template to create an infographic about themselves, including information about their families, interests, and future goals. This project introduces students to the designs, elements, and text features available in Canva, which is free for all K–12 teachers. My students use Canva to design slides for various projects and host our student websites.

2. **Identity presentation:** Students transfer the information from their infographic into a preferred presentation platform. Creators get to decide how best to divide their personal stories on separate slides, and they begin familiarizing themselves with tools like animations and transitions that bring their presentations to life. Students can also record audio and video for their presentations and enjoy each other's presentations in a gallery stroll.

3. **The Writer of This Poem:** This activity is inspired by a poem of the same name by Roger McGough (2005). Students fill in the poem graphic organizer (figure 1.6) using the parts of speech organizer (figure 1.7, page 28) on paper and then fill in the blanks on the word processing document in their digital folder for this project. Creators then practice using the various word processor design features, such as fonts, text colors, backgrounds, borders, and so on.

---

**The Writer of This Poem**   by _____

The writer of this poem

Is as _____1_____ as a _____1_____
As _____2_____ as a _____2_____
As _____3_____ as can be

The writer of this poem

Is a _____10_____
That _____8_____ like a _____8_____
And is _____4_____ like a _____4_____

This writer is as _____11_____
As _____5_____ as a _____5_____
That cries out _____9_____ into the _____9_____
And is _____6_____ like a _____6_____

The writer of this poem
Is amazing as can be
_____Name_____ is _____7_____ as a _____7_____
(or so the teacher says!)

---

*Source: McGough, 2005.*

**FIGURE 1.6:** *Poem graphic organizer.*

*Visit **go.SolutionTree.com/technology** for a free reproducible version of this figure.*

1. List seven positive adjectives that describe you and seven other things those adjectives might also be used to describe.

| | Adjective | Noun that adjective also describes |
|---|---|---|
| 1. | | |
| 2. | | |
| 3. | | |
| 4. | | |
| 5. | | |
| 6. | | |
| 7. | | |

2. Pick a verb that you often do and another thing in the world that would perform the same action.

| | Verb | Noun that would also use that verb |
|---|---|---|
| 8. | | |

3. Pick an exclamation that you might shout and the place where you would be shouting it.

| | Exclamation | Place where you would be shouting |
|---|---|---|
| 9. | | |

4. Pick two nouns that could be used as metaphors to describe you.

| | Noun |
|---|---|
| 10. | |
| 11. | |

**FIGURE 1.7:** Parts of speech organizer.

Visit **go.SolutionTree.com/technology** *for a free reproducible version of this figure.*

By enlisting your mavens in these projects, you honor students' expertise by entrusting them with leadership opportunities throughout the creative process.

### Allow Speech-to-Text

Every year, I have students in my classroom who, for a multitude of reasons, cannot type on a computer keyboard. When I began teaching, I made students muscle through; since then, every word processor and presentation software includes a dictate function that allows student creators to author their content using speech-to-text. Many educators resist students utilizing this tool because they recognize the importance of students learning to type. However, when empowering students' voices is the goal, allowing them to use those same voices to generate text for their projects makes perfect sense.

### Utilize Translation Tools

I teach in a beautifully diverse, culturally rich Title I school, and the number of students who don't speak English as their first language increases each year. While most search engines, generative AI, and other online tools can facilitate translations for users, many word processors and presentation platforms have built-in tools that can translate selected text or entire documents into different languages and dialects. Multilingual creators can use this feature to type their content in their native language and then translate it into English. Students can also fine-tune these program's language settings by selecting their home language as the document's primary language. This setting change affects spelling and grammar checks, and it can help multilingual learners identify their own errors more effectively.

### Select the Easiest Option

When creators record their presentations as webinars, different computer programs boast different capabilities. For example, if your students use PowerPoint, they can record their presentation—either from start to finish or one slide at a time—right there in the program. If your students instead use a platform like Google Slides that doesn't allow them to record within the program itself (as of this writing), you'll need to either use a screen recorder or a video conferencing platform to capture their presentation. Again, the tools I use are listed in figure 1.6 (page 27), and there are countless tutorials available to help your creators make the most of these programs. My rule of thumb when selecting options for these projects is simple—the easiest option wins. Whichever tool captures your students' performances in the fewest steps, makes the most sense, and intimidates you the least, is the way to go.

## Amplifying Student Voices

The fun really starts once students finish their digital projects. Whether they publish their blog posts or upload their presentations online, your young creators are finally ready to share their creations with the world.

First, as discussed in the introduction (page 3), make sure you're consistently communicating with your administrators and students' parents from the start of any digital project. Next, make sure everyone in your class has returned their signed media release form. Finally, decide on an online platform dedicated to sharing your students' finished products. For blog posts and recorded presentations, my favorite option is for each student to post their work on their very own website. The following sections detail some useful information about class and student websites, as well as some ideal podcasting platforms.

### Class and Student Websites

The two programs I prefer for creating class or student websites are Canva and Google Sites. If you're new to this, begin by building a test run class website using one of these two tools; both are free to use and easily accessible for teachers and students. If you're not sure which to pick, the following are some of the pros and cons for both platforms.

- **Google Sites pros:**
    - *Free and easy to use*—It's a free website builder with a user-friendly interface, making it accessible for students with varying technical skills as burgeoning web developers.
    - *Integration with Google Workspace*—It integrates with other Google tools like Google Docs and Slides, allowing documents and presentations to be easily embedded into the website.
    - *Collaboration*—Google Sites allows multiple users to collaborate on the same website simultaneously, making it ideal for group projects or if your creators want to host shared work together.
    - *Customizable design*—Templates and customization options are available for students to personalize their website's design, layout, and color scheme.
    - *Secure hosting*—Google Sites provides secure hosting, safeguarding your students' data and privacy.
- **Google Sites con:**
    - *Design options*—Google Sites is limited in the number of customizable design options compared with Canva.
- **Canva pros:**
    - *Design focused*—Canva is known for its wide range of design templates, graphics, fonts, and images, making it ideal for young creators interested in visually appealing and professional-looking websites.
    - *User-friendly*—Its drag-and-drop interface and predesigned templates make Canva beginner friendly, enabling students without technical knowledge to successfully create visually appealing websites.
    - *Collaboration*—Like Google Sites, Canva allows users to share and collaborate on website projects with others, making it awesome for group projects.
    - *Content creation options*—Canva allows easy creation and customization of images, infographics, charts, and other visual content that students can use on their webpages.
    - *Integration with other tools*—It integrates with popular platforms like Dropbox, Google Drive, and Pexels, providing access to a vast library of stock photos and illustrations for young creators' websites and digital projects.
- **Canva con:**
    - *Limited structuring and navigation options*—It can be challenging to create and organize hierarchical website structures as opposed to Google Sites.

## *Podcasting Platforms*

When considering the best options for posting your students' podcasts, it really comes down to two choices: using a learning management system like Canvas or Moodle versus a podcast hosting platform like Simplecast or Libsyn. The choice should align with your instructional goals and resources, as well as your students' technical proficiency and desired audience. Some teachers use both options, posting content first on their learning management system for easy access and then podcast hosting platforms for broader distribution. The following are some pros and cons for each of these options.

- Learning management system pros:
  - **Control:** Hosting podcasts on your school or district's learning management system allows for greater control and ownership of your students' digital content.
  - **Privacy:** You can maintain better control of your students' data privacy and security of student content.
  - **Easy approval:** School leaders and parents already approve these platforms, so you don't have to secure permission to post student work elsewhere.
  - **Integration:** Integrating student podcasts with existing coursework and materials you have already posted on the learning management system is easier.
  - **Cost-effective:** Hosting on school or district servers should be free.
- Learning management system cons:
  - **Limited distribution:** Student's content can only be viewed by others with access to the learning management system.
  - **Long buffer times:** Learning management systems are designed to deal with text rather than large audio and video files, so endless loading and buffering may become frustrating over time.
- Podcast hosting platform pros:
  - **User-friendly:** Podcast hosting platforms are designed to be user-friendly, making it easy for your students to upload and manage their podcast episodes.
  - **Distribution:** These platforms have built-in distribution to major podcast directories like Apple Podcasts and Spotify, ensuring a wide potential reach for your students' content.
  - **Analytics:** You and your students can track the number of clicks, downloads, and other performance indicators their podcasts receive.
  - **Customization:** Students can create customizable podcast profiles and channels to give their work a professional look.
  - **Simplified RSS feeds:** A really simple syndication (RSS) feed helps users keep track of updates to their favorite websites, podcasts, blogs, and so on, in a single online news aggregator. Hosting platforms generate RSS feeds automatically, eliminating this technical barrier for students.
- Podcast hosting platform cons:
  - **Cost and data privacy issues:** Many podcast hosting platforms come with a cost. However, there are free options like Spotify for Podcasters, and if the teacher owns the podcast account and simply uploads student audio files as episodes, then their data privacy is secured.

## Conclusion

Once student work is posted online, embrace the immense joy and heavy responsibility that comes with amplifying your students' voices. What should you, as their teacher, do with their content? Post it on your class website? Disseminate links among your colleagues and professional networks? Share their pieces on your own social media channels?

As a great teacher once told me, the only right answer is *it all depends*. It depends on the comfort level of their parents and your school. It depends on the themes and messages in your students' work and which audiences need to see their pieces the most. Most importantly, it depends on how public facing each student wants their own work to be. You shouldn't share work that students want to hold close; at the same time, once content is posted on the internet, young creators need to know they can only hold on so tight before that content goes *everywhere*. If students don't want the whole world to see their products, they can keep their work privately posted so only those they trust with the link will be able to access it. Meanwhile, other students will post their pieces on Instagram as soon as they publish it. The point of empowering student voices is to give them as much control over their creative works as any adult would insist on for themselves.

My students know that if their finished project might be inspiring or instructive for others to see, I'm going to share it with as many people as I possibly can. My students also know that I will always ask for their permission first. And when I ask, "Is it OK for me to share your incredible work?" they usually blush at the sight of pride in my eyes.

# CHAPTER 2

# Blog Posts

**PROJECT OBJECTIVE**
I will empower my students' voices by teaching them to share their writing with an online audience of readers.

Definition of **blog**

**noun**
A website that contains online personal reflections, comments, and often hyperlinks, videos, and photographs provided by the writer.

**verb**
To write or have a blog.

—Merriam-Webster Online Dictionary

## CREATORS AT WORK

"But how do I get the reader to read it the way I want them to?" Brendan moaned as I knelt beside him.

Brendan once cried in the middle of class because I made him slow down and follow the steps in a long division problem. It wasn't mathematics that made him cry—he was meticulous and loved solving problems. It was slowing down that made him sad.

"What do you mean, *the way I want them to*?" I asked.

Brendan was on our sixth-grade debate team, and he had written an argumentative speech months before on the federal government's role in education. When I informed the class that, for this digital project, they would be transforming a previous expository writing assignment into their website's first blog post, he knew exactly which one to pick.

"I mean, even if they're reading in their brains, I want them to pause for effect like I do here after the word *show*, and I want them to really emphasize *the government doesn't want that to happen* and not just trail off at the end of the sentence."

Brendan had spent months preparing his speech and performance for the judges, and his greatest fear was that someone would read his blog post online and not like it because they read it "wrong."

I pointed at the blog post rubric beside his computer, which is illustrated in figure 2.1 (page 35). I said, "Look where it says *Writing Conventions*. 'The post's grammar, punctuation, and text features are used effectively to enhance the content and communicate the author's voice.' What that means is a strong writer deliberately uses commas, dashes, bold, italics, and so on, to make the words on the page read exactly how they would if *you* were saying them out loud."

We spent the next five minutes adding commas where he wanted the reader to pause, ellipses where he wanted them to linger, and triple emphasis to "*The government doesn't want that to happen!*"

I then continued by saying, "You can't make eye *contact* with your audience in a blog post, but you can make your content eye *catching*. You can use different colors, images, and fonts to make your piece more engaging and enjoyable for your reader. However, it's like seasoning a dish—too much or too little can ruin the whole experience. Strike a balance, be tasteful, and remember—"

"I know, I know, I know," Brendan said. "No weird cursive fonts."

"Or multicolored backgrounds because—"

"Readability is *everything*," he answered, right on cue.

---

**OF ALL THE DIGITAL** projects shared in this book, blogs have the lowest entry point and highest ceiling for students and teachers entering this new digital landscape. Across all content areas, students can easily transform any expository or narrative writing assignment into a blog post simply by publishing it on a class or student website.

*Blogs*, a contraction of *web* and *log*, are websites used to publish writing in a variety of nonfiction formats and may include graphics, multimedia, or hyperlinks to other websites (Richardson, 2010). There are five key features of blogs: (1) personal editorship, (2) a hyperlinked post structure, (3) frequent updates, (4) free public access to the content online, and (5) archived postings (Paquet, 2002). Essentially, a blog post is written, shared, updated, and often connected through links to other works that inform it. In the education field, blogs used for teaching and learning purposes, also called *edublogs*, have gained popularity and are used to promote the innovative learning styles of digital-generation students (Zhang, Song, Shen, & Huang, 2014).

Students first need to understand the characteristics and components of a well-written blog before beginning their projects. Providing model blog posts for students to evaluate with the blog post rubric (figure 2.1) is a great way to clarify your expectations for students' writing and what success can look like on this project.

The following are some model blogs for students.

- **Youth Voices (www.youthvoices.live):** Organized by teachers with support from the National Writing Project, Youth Voices is an open-publishing and social-networking platform for students and teachers to creatively explore topics together through blog and discussion posts.
- **Fifth Grade (https://mooreclassmath.edublogs.org):** This fifth-grade classroom blog provides students with a platform for sharing their perspectives on life, both in and out of school. This blog also provides links to other useful resources for teachers interested in starting their own classroom blogs.
- **Fanschool (https://fan.school/spaces?spaceId=y3xUrnZHvGAEqMI1KSXB):** Fanschool is a safe and social learning network where young people can create digital portfolios and blogs. The collection of posts in this source is from authors and educators in the Fanschool community who believe in improving instructional practices and transferring ownership of learning to students.

| | 3 | 2 | 1 |
|---|---|---|---|
| **Content** | The post presents a focused, engaging, and original message or idea. The post is logically organized, with relevant and interesting supporting details throughout. | The post presents a broad message or idea. The post is loosely organized, with supporting details that are somewhat relevant and connected throughout. | The post's message or idea is unclear. The post lacks organization with few or no relevant details. |
| **Voice** | The post is written in a distinctive, compelling voice that draws in the reader and reflects the author's unique style or perspective. The post makes effective use of tone, word choice, figurative language, and sensory details. | The post is written in a voice that communicates a general perspective to the reader. The post makes some use of tone, word choice, figurative language, and sensory details. | The post is written in an indistinct voice and fails to communicate the author's perspective. The post makes almost no use of tone, word choice, figurative language, or sensory details. |
| **Writing Conventions** | The post is free of grammar, spelling, or punctuation errors. The post's grammar, punctuation, and text features are used effectively to enhance the content and communicate the author's voice. | The post includes some grammar, spelling, or punctuation errors. The post's grammar, punctuation, and text features somewhat support the content and reading. | The post contains numerous grammar, spelling, or punctuation errors. The post's grammar, punctuation, and text features interfere with the content and author's voice. |
| **Layout and Graphics** | The blog's features, like graphics, photos, and multimedia, are inserted when appropriate to enhance the post's visual appeal and readability. The post correctly acknowledges all image and multimedia sources with captions or annotations. | The blog's features, like graphics, photos, and multimedia, are included in the post. The post acknowledges some image and multimedia sources with captions or annotations. | The blog's features, like graphics, photos, and multimedia, are not included or do little to enhance the post. The post does not acknowledge image and multimedia sources with captions or annotations. |
| **Blogging Conventions** | The post is categorized, and topics are tagged appropriately, making it easy for the user to locate on the site. (Optional) The post contains embedded external links to sources or internal links situating it within the author's larger network of posts. | The post is loosely categorized and tagged, making it somewhat difficult to locate. (Optional) The post contains few embedded external links to sources or internal links situating it within the author's larger network of posts. | The post is not categorized or tagged. (Optional) The post contains no embedded external links to sources or internal links situating it within the author's larger network of posts. |

**FIGURE 2.1:** *Blog post rubric.*

*Visit **go.SolutionTree.com/technology** for a free reproducible version of this figure.*

## The Project

In this project, students will write a blog post intended for an online audience of readers. This is the digital project I start with each school year because it taps into skills my students have already developed in prior grades, while also introducing new tools and showing young creators the value and potential reach of their work.

Figure 2.2 outlines the steps my students follow to successfully complete this digital project. Whether a student is adapting a previously written piece into a blog post or writing original work for their blog, the five stages of the writing process remain the same: (1) prewrite, (2) draft, (3) revise, (4) proofread, and (5) publish. For this project, each stage comes with a series of steps (detailed in the following sections), such as brainstorming and researching during the prewriting stage. However, if a student is adapting a previously written work, they can skip down to the revise stage (step 5) and begin revising with an online audience in mind.

| Blogger: | Title of Blog Post: | Date: |
|---|---|---|

| **Prewrite** |
|---|
| Step 1: Brainstorm ideas and select a topic of interest. |
| Topic: _____ |
| Step 2: Research information, images, and interesting facts about the topic. |
| **Draft** |
| Step 3: Outline the blog post. |
| Step 4: Type a draft of the blog post, including any images and graphics you intend to use. |
| **Revise** |
| Step 5: Score the blog post with the rubric. Revise as needed. |
| Step 6: Have at least two critical friends score your blog post with the rubric and fill out a Critical Friend Feedback Form. Revise as needed. |
| Step 7: Conference with the teacher. Revise as needed. |
| **Proofread** |
| Step 8: Edit the blog post, correcting for any remaining errors in writing/blogging conventions. |
| Step 9: Test all embedded links and check the blog post's webpage layout. |
| **Publish** |
| Step 10: Publish the blog post online and complete an After-Project Reflection. |

**FIGURE 2.2:** Blog post planning.

Visit **go.SolutionTree.com/technology** for a free reproducible version of this figure.

### Prewrite

Prewriting is the critical first step in writing an effective blog post. Like drawing a blueprint before building a house, it's the stage where ideas percolate, a framework takes shape, and syntactic structures begin to form.

Clarity is one of the main benefits of prewriting for student blogs. As students brainstorm ideas, choose their topics, and research their selections, young creators gain a clearer understanding of their message and target audience. This clarity enhances the content's quality and facilitates a smoother drafting and revision process, reducing the students' chances of veering off topic or losing reader interest. Moreover, prewriting encourages exploration and experimentation, allowing writers to dig into various perspectives, points of view, and nuances related to their topic.

My best advice is don't rush the prewriting process; prewriting should allow students enough time to refine their authorial voice and give you the time needed to perform quality checks on their ideas and topics for coherence, relevance, and audience engagement.

### Step 1: Brainstorm Ideas and Select a Topic of Interest

Students begin this project like any other—by brainstorming topics and selecting a focus. I know you probably have specific prompts, topics, and questions that you love using to guide your students' writing throughout the year, and I want you to bring those same prompts to this project. However, as much as possible, I also encourage you to free your students to write about what they find most compelling *in the content that you teach*. When students make decisions about their work, they are empowered to own it; that ownership leads to self-direction, self-discipline, motivation, and a personal investment in the project's outcome (Dabrowski & Marshall, 2018). To help my creators select topics that matter to them, I provide them each with the blog post topic selection page shown in figure 2.3.

---

**Brainstorm**

1. What topic would you be most excited to explore in your blog post? Explain why.

2. What message would you like to explore and communicate in your blog post?

3. Who would be the intended audience for your blog post? Explain why.

4. What would be your purpose in writing this blog post (to inform, raise awareness, or create change)? How would you achieve that purpose?

---

**FIGURE 2.3:** *Blog post topic selection.*

*Visit **go.SolutionTree.com/technology** for a free reproducible version of this figure.*

One of the most rewarding practices in a teacher's toolbox is connecting class content with meaningful, real-world applications. For example, the first mathematics concept I teach each school year is ratios; if I told my students on the first day that they'd all be writing blog posts about ratios, they might throw me right out the window—if they were feeling especially generous, they might open it first. However, if I told them they could write a blog post about any topic they find super interesting but they must thoughtfully incorporate at least five ratio relationships into their post, then they're suddenly applying the mathematical concept I need them to master in a language arts project for an online audience.

Let's say a student chose to write about homelessness. A ratio relationship they might include is the number of available beds in shelters in Salt Lake City to the number of people without houses. Connecting content to the topics your students care about—and then providing platforms for them to address their concerns—is among the most effective means for bringing purpose and meaning to your students' everyday work.

### Step 2: Research Information, Images, and Interesting Facts About the Topic

Once your students know what they want to blog about, it's time for them to start researching. Of course, this will look different depending on their grade level, the content you teach, and the availability of books and online research tools you have in your classroom.

Chapter 1 (page 13) provides several resources and lesson ideas for teaching media literacy and finding credible, reliable sources online. I suggest having students do all their research online for this project because they can copy article and website links for their sources into a word processor document and later embed them directly into their blog posts, saving them the trouble of going back and locating the bibliographic information.

Students always ask, "How much research do I need to do?" Here's my answer: "If you have five fascinating facts in your presentation—five compelling pieces of information you can share with your audience that they might not already know—then high-five! You're crushing the research game."

To support this requirement and ensure students understand they must acquire and show these facts before moving on to outlining their presentations, you can provide them with a "Five Fascinating Facts" sheet found in the appendix (page 156). This step ensures you can confirm they have indeed selected fascinating and relevant evidence for their topic and theme.

### Draft

Drafting is the next step in producing a published blog post. It's where the raw materials gathered during prewriting begin to take shape as a cogent argument or compelling statement. When drafting, students flesh out ideas, refine language, and experiment with different structures and styles. In the context of content creation, drafting provides young creators with low-stakes opportunities to take big creative swings and endure embarrassing misses, iterating nonstop and failing forward throughout. Ultimately, our goal is to support students in refining their work, ensuring that each point they make flows logically to the next. By embracing the drafting process, you will help your students produce content that captivates and inspires their readers.

### Step 3: Outline the Blog Post

Having students outline their work before they begin drafting comes with an incredibly high return on investment. Whether they scribble their bullet-pointed thoughts onto scratch paper or thoroughly detail their work in a graphic organizer, outlining helps students develop their central theme or *throughline*, identify the new idea or original insight they hope to communicate, gather the most relevant and useful information related to their topic, and organize their ideas in a sequential manner with a logical flow. In my class, every student must fill out the blog post outline shown in figure 2.4 before they can begin drafting. Only after I have reviewed a student's outline and provided feedback do I give them the go-ahead to begin writing their draft; this added step saves time in the long run, because nothing delays completion more than a student needing to change course mid-project.

| **Blogger:** | **Blog Post Title:** | **Date:** |
|---|---|---|
| Throughline: <br><br> What is the connecting theme or central idea of your blog post? | | |
| Message: <br><br> What message are you communicating to your audience? | | |
| Introduction: | | |
| Body: | | |
| Conclusion: | | |

**FIGURE 2.4:** *Blog post outline.*

*Visit* **go.SolutionTree.com/technology** *for a free reproducible version of this figure.*

### Step 4: Type a Draft of the Blog Post

The necessary content of each blog post is there in the rubric outline; however, I can begin assessing my students' writing for voice, writing conventions, and layout and graphics once I have a typed draft in hand.

My sixth graders typically aren't the strongest typists, so I have them compose on paper before typing their drafts. And because I'm already familiar with each student's central idea, key details, and research from their outline, what I'm looking for in their typed drafts is elaboration: Have they fully fleshed out their central idea in a new and interesting way? Have they effectively buttressed their argument with strong supporting details? Is their writing voice distinctive and compelling? Do the graphics included in the post clarify and contribute to the message the author is trying to convey? No matter the answer, the real work of addressing these questions comes in the next stage.

## Revise

Of all the writing-process stages, the revision phase is the most involved. This is where students take a step back to evaluate their work and support their classmates in doing the same. The best part of this revision process is how self-aware writers become as they assess their own work objectively and identify areas for improvement. By self-reflecting on their work, reviewing their writing with peers, and conferencing with their teacher—the master in the room—creators will be best equipped to elevate the overall quality of their content. I've always found that the more people you can get to read a piece prior to publishing, the better the final product will be.

### Step 5: Score the Blog Post With the Rubric and Revise

I begin by having my students evaluate their own drafts using the blog post rubric featured in figure 2.1 (page 35). This rubric empowers them to self-identify areas they feel need the most improvements and revisions. I love watching my students go back and forth between their pieces and the rubric, assigning themselves either a three, two, or one in each category. Students will sometimes ask if they need to write notes on the rubric explaining why they gave themselves the score they did. I tell them that the rubric is a tool to help them see their own writing through the eyes of an online reader, and the notes I'm looking for will be in the revisions they make between this draft and the next.

### Step 6: Peer Review the Blog Post and Revise Based on Feedback

Once students finish evaluating and revising their draft, they must elicit feedback from at least two critical friends, who each score the blog post with the rubric and fill out the "Critical Friend Feedback Form" in figure 2.5 (and in the appendix on page 157).

I describe a *critical friend* to my students as a fellow creator you trust to provide honest insights and useful critiques of your work. The best critical friends delicately balance support and candor as they reveal what students can't see in their own writing—blind spots, weaknesses, and their awesome strengths. As discussed in the introduction (page 3), creating a classroom environment where students feel safe and supported and where they can give each other constructive and honest feedback takes time and intention. So, for this project, assume that work has been done and students are ready to give and receive positive and productive suggestions for improving their pieces. This feedback can be collected in a variety of ways, but here are three of my favorite structures for engaging critical friends.

---

**Critical Friend Feedback Form**

A critical friend is a classmate who is committed to helping you improve as a content creator. A critical friend is encouraging and supportive, and they can be trusted to provide constructive, honest feedback on specific ways you can improve your work.

| Critical Friend: | Content Creator: | Project Title: |
| --- | --- | --- |

I Like . . .

_____

_____

I Wonder . . .

_____

_____

I Suggest . . .

_____

_____

---

**FIGURE 2.5:** *Critical friend feedback form.*

- Tape up all drafts around the room and have students select pieces to evaluate in a gallery stroll. This is a fun and engaging way to get students up and moving while also giving them the chance to see everyone else's work.
- Randomly distribute two drafts for each student to evaluate. The critical friend writes their name on their feedback form, but I like to keep the identity of each author anonymous during this activity because it helps the evaluator remain unbiased. Plus, they get to guess who the writer is based solely on the voice.
- Let students select their own reviewers—classmates they trust to give them the feedback they need to meaningfully improve their work.

### Step 7: Conference With the Teacher and Revise

There is an old saying passed down by wise veteran educators to first-year teachers—*three before me*. At this stage in the process, three sets of eyes have provided feedback on each student's work, and the writer has revised their pieces accordingly. Now is the time for students to conference with you individually as you look at their blog posts together.

I like to begin with a quick comparison of their original draft with their revised draft, examining the changes they made after scoring their own work and receiving feedback from their critical friends. Then, I share with them what I like about their piece, wonder about, and suggest for future revisions. These are powerful conversations to have with students, but it's important to keep them quick; the only way to reasonably visit with each student is to do so with focus and efficiency. Spend no more than ten minutes with each student.

### *Proofread*

After conferencing with you, have students revise their pieces one more time, and then—huzzah! The hard work of creating original and engaging content is done. But before they publish their work online, each writer must carefully proofread their piece, ensuring they haven't missed any glaring grammatical or technical errors. Students also use this time to check every embedded link and finalize their layout for online publication. By meticulously proofreading their work for mistakes and inconsistencies, young creators develop a keen eye for detail and a commitment to excellence in their products.

### *Step 8: Edit the Blog Post, Correcting for Any Remaining Errors*

Beyond the word processor's grammar and spell checks, my district provides students with an online proofreading tool to find and correct writing errors. If your school or district does not, there are free online proofreading tools like Grammarly that will check your students' work and provide them with corrective feedback. While these tools can be helpful, they rely on AI to generate correction suggestions and, therefore, sometimes provide false suggestions that fail to consider context and voice.

### *Step 9: Test All Embedded Links and Check the Blog Post's Webpage Layout*

This should be the quickest stage of the process, and yet, due to the often glitchy nature of class or student-run websites, students can easily get caught in the quicksand of webpage formatting issues. We spend so much time teaching students to color within the lines that they grow up to become adolescents who can't stand text that's even slightly off-center or photographs that aren't sized quite right. Save them from themselves—limit the amount of time students have to format their posts to thirty minutes.

### *Publish*

Finally, your students' blog posts are ready to be published online. No matter which platform you're using or whether you or your students are pushing the publish button, their work will be accessible to individuals beyond the walls of your classroom. This is a time of careful consideration for young creators, reflecting on the process that brought them to this moment, the level of interaction they want to have with their pieces now that they're published, and how they can further improve their work going forward.

### *Step 10: Publish the Blog Post Online and Complete an After-Project Reflection*

You might imagine that, once a student's blog post is published online, the work is done; if that's as far as you want to take this project, that's great. However, there are opportunities at this point in the process for students to shift their focus from creation to audience engagement and reflection.

First, depending on how the website or digital portfolio is set up, readers may be able to leave comments for student bloggers on their work. This feedback from readers around the world can be thrilling, instructive, and impactful for students in ways unparalleled by anything else in the classroom. The desire to satisfy and continue engaging with their audience can compel students to revise and update their posts long after a project is finished or a grade has been assigned. Also, if a student's writing touches on a current event or controversial issue, engaging with their post may elevate their voice into a larger conversation of local, national, or international importance.

At the same time, knowing that our students' work is on the internet and susceptible to attacks and internet trolls is a scary thought for any parent, administrator, or classroom teacher. Teachers can help everyone rest easier by selecting a platform for hosting their class or student websites that allows them to review and remove inappropriate content before it's available for all to see. And again, as I mentioned in the introduction (page 3), make sure you have all your media release forms turned in, do all you can to safeguard your students' identities and intellectual property, and keep everyone well-informed throughout the creative process.

Finally, before your digital content creators move on to their next project, it's important for them reflect on their performance as first-time bloggers. By completing the "After-Project Reflection Form" (page 158 in the appendix), students can examine what they liked and appreciated in their own work, what they could have improved by making different choices, and what they will do moving forward to take their creative process and work products to the next level.

## Conclusion

I like to imagine that you've reached the end of this chapter twice. The first time you read it, you immediately jumped out of bed and added *blogging* to all your lesson plans. Now, a week or two later, you're reading through it a second time because your students' blogs are either going extremely well or you're looking for some help.

Either way, let's revisit the chapter-opening objective for this project: *I will empower my students' voices by teaching them to share their writing with an online audience of readers.* That's it—you're here because you know your students have important things to say, and you want them to reach as many people as possible. There are lots of simple ways to achieve this objective, so if this project is feeling a little overwhelming, here are a few other options for amplifying your students' voices:

- Post their written pieces on your own social media platforms and encourage your friends to share. You still need students' permission to remove any identifying information, of course, but posting on social media is a quick and easy way to disseminate their work to a broader online audience.

- Submit their writing to blogs run by other people. Many popular blogs, online journals, and so on, accept submissions from writers hoping to publish on their platforms. Finding a blog that accepts student submissions and already has an established audience makes life a whole lot easier for you.

- Send in their pieces as letters to the editors of local or national newspapers. If selected, not only would their pieces be published and shared online, but they might also come away with a newspaper clipping of their work—a quaint and lovely souvenir in this increasingly digital world.

# CHAPTER 3
# Presentations

**PROJECT OBJECTIVE**
I will empower my students' voices by teaching them to share thoughtfully crafted presentations with an online audience of viewers.

**Definition of Present**

**verb**
To bring before the public or to one's attention.
To bring or introduce into the presence of someone.
To introduce socially.

—Merriam-Webster Online Dictionary

## CREATORS AT WORK

"Believe me, I know you're sick of hearing me say this, but I'm still going to say it one more time: in order to *present*, you have to *be present*."

Annie nodded, having just finished rehearsing her presentation, then mumbled something I couldn't quite hear.

"What was that?"

"I said, I am present."

From the back of my classroom, I still had to strain to hear her. She had a microphone, but Annie kept it hovering just above her belly button. "No, you're not. You're reading your speech so fast because you want it to end as quickly as possible. You're not staying present in *this* moment we're sharing together, in which you are gifting me with this idea and information, and I am gifting you with my undivided attention. Staying present means you stand up straight, maintain eye contact, take my metaphorical hand, and guide me through this incredible presentation about why teachers need to listen to their students more."

A few weeks earlier, Annie had tapped me on the shoulder and asked, "We can really make a presentation about *anything*?" When I reassured her that I meant what I'd said, she asked, "Well, what if I want to make a presentation listing all the reasons teachers should listen to what their students have to say?"

I must have chuckled or something, because Annie said, "I'm serious!"

"I know you are, and I promise I am, too. If you make a presentation convincing me and every other teacher that we need to listen more to our students, you'll make me the happiest teacher in the world."

And she did. Ten-year-old Annie found fascinating evidence to support her claim that all kids need to be listened to, especially our youngest. Her research showed that, in some studies, four- and five-year-olds have outsmarted college students in determining how new toys and gadgets work, and preschoolers have figured out how to activate machines with unusual objects faster than adults. Annie's slide presentation was a thing of beauty; however, when she began rehearsing her presentation, that fearless young lady wandered off, and a shy, bashful child stepped into her shoes.

I crossed the room, showed Annie the presentation rubric from figure 3.1, and said, "Check this out: in terms of your content, writing conventions, and layout and graphics, you're already scoring perfect threes. But look down here at physicality and voice; remember that the word *dynamic* appears in both top-scoring boxes. Dynamic means you are constantly bringing energy into your physical and vocal performance throughout your presentation. I know it's awkward right now, but when you're up here, you want to engage your classmates with your hands and your eyes. You want to thoughtfully take your voice for a bit of a ride—higher, lower, faster, slower. The words are all there. We just need to juice up your performance!"

That day, she would have scored ones for voice and physicality, for sure. But when she presented in front of our class a week later after reflecting on the feedback and practicing more, she received twos in both categories from me and most of her classmates.

Scan the QR code to see Annie's presentation; my favorite line is her very last—"listening equals learning for teachers, too."

**THIS DIGITAL PROJECT WILL** delve into the art of presenting and public speaking, guiding students through each essential step in the process. As teachers, we recognize the importance of equipping our students with effective communication skills and providing them with platforms to express their thoughts, ideas, and opinions in a compelling and impactful manner. However, helping students recognize the necessity of learning to speak in public is probably my hardest struggle as a teacher each year. I hate making students cry, and yet I have at least one student every year who cries real tears when it's time to speak in front of the class.

I'll talk about specific strategies for public speaking in this chapter, but there are two things I give my students to mitigate their fears about presenting in front of their peers: (1) options for presenting and (2) opportunities to practice.

There are many different types of digital presentations students can deliver in class (slide decks, slideshows, and so on) and variations within each type. For example, I prefer that my students create PowerPoint presentations because it's the platform I'm most comfortable with. However, sometimes students come into class already adept at using Prezi, and they prefer creating their content in that more dynamic landscape. That's great, too!

|  | 3 | 2 | 1 |
|---|---|---|---|
| **Content** | The presentation shares a focused, engaging, and original message or idea.<br><br>The presentation is logically organized, with relevant and interesting details throughout. | The presentation shares a broad message or idea.<br><br>The presentation is loosely organized, with details that are somewhat relevant and connected throughout. | The presentation's message or idea is unclear.<br><br>The presentation lacks organization, with few or no relevant details. |
| **Writing Conventions** | The text and speech are free of grammatical, spelling, or punctuation errors.<br><br>The grammar, punctuation, and text features effectively enhance the content and communicate the presenter's ideas. | The text and speech include some grammatical, spelling, or punctuation errors.<br><br>The grammar, punctuation, and text features somewhat enhance the content and communicate the presenter's ideas. | The text and speech contain numerous grammatical, spelling, or punctuation errors.<br><br>The grammar, punctuation, and text features interfere with the content and ideas in the presentation. |
| **Layout and Graphics** | The presentation effectively uses visual aids or multimedia to enhance understanding and engagement with the content.<br><br>The presentation makes great use of transitions, animations, and other design features to engage the audience. | The presentation occasionally uses visual aids or multimedia to support understanding and engagement with the content.<br><br>The presentation makes good use of transitions, animations, and other design features to engage the audience. | The presentation does not effectively utilize visual aids or multimedia to enhance understanding or engagement with the content.<br><br>The presentation uses distracting transitions, animations, and other design features. |
| **Presentation:**<br>**Physicality**<br>**Posture**<br>**Gestures**<br>**Eye Contact**<br>**Facial Expressions**<br>**Movement** | The presenter engages the audience with a confident and dynamic physical performance, enhancing their presentation with gestures, facial expressions, and movements.<br><br>The presenter maintains strong posture and eye contact with the audience. | The presenter engages the audience with a physical performance that incorporates some gestures, facial expressions, and movements.<br><br>The presenter maintains good posture and some eye contact with the audience. | The presenter struggles to engage the audience with the physical performance due to weak posture and few gestures, facial expressions, or movements.<br><br>The presenter has weak posture and little eye contact with the audience. |
| **Presentation:**<br>**Voice**<br>**Volume**<br>**Tone**<br>**Modulation**<br>**Energy**<br>**Enthusiasm** | The presenter engages the audience with a confident and dynamic speaking style.<br><br>The presenter speaks clearly and enunciates throughout the presentation. | The presenter engages the audience with an adequate speaking style, but occasional hesitations or lack of confidence are noticeable.<br><br>The presenter speaks somewhat clearly and enunciates at times. | The presenter struggles to engage the audience due to weak speaking style, hesitations, lack of confidence, or monotone delivery.<br><br>The presenter's speech is muffled and difficult to understand. |

**FIGURE 3.1:** *Presentation rubric.*

*Visit **go.SolutionTree.com/technology** for a free reproducible version of this figure.*

Some students enjoy the freedom of delivering their presentations for however long and with any number of slides, while others prefer a more structured format like PechaKucha (*chit-chat* in Japanese), which consists of twenty slides shown for twenty seconds each (Liao et al., 2020). Because of the time constraint, students are forced to streamline their presentations, make thoughtful decisions about what slides they will or won't include, and practice multiple times in advance of their class performance. So, before launching into this project, think about what format for designing and delivering digital presentations makes the most sense for you and your students. Then, give them lots of time to rehearse individually, with critical friends (as described in chapter 2, page 33), and at least once with you.

I'll also review different options for recording and sharing these presentations with friends, family, and a broader online audience. From capturing their live performance on your smartphone to Zoom recording their presentation as a webinar, we will look at all the ways you can disseminate the ideas and messages in your students' presentations into the world.

During my second year of teaching, I created a digital presentation called *Why We Learn* that I still deliver imperfectly each year for my students. They watch me with rubrics in hand, and after I finish, I draw a feedback T-chart (see figure 3.2) on the board and ask my students, "What did you appreciate about this presentation and performance, and what can I, as a presenter, improve going forward?"

| **Basic Feedback** | **Positive and Productive Feedback** |
|---|---|
| I couldn't hear you. | If you speak louder, your voice will be clearer, easier to understand, and more engaging to listen to. |
| I like your pictures. | I really like how your visuals brought us into the landscape you described! |
| Your introduction was good. | Your introduction was captivating and grabbed my attention right away. No cap! ["No lie!"] |
| You didn't look up the whole time. | When you present again, making eye contact throughout your performance will help keep the audience interested. |

**FIGURE 3.2:** *Feedback T-chart.*

We discuss and evaluate my presentation together one criterion at a time, and as each student shares, we take what they say and translate it into two types of feedback: (1) basic feedback or (2) positive and productive feedback. For folks of my generation, if you hear a student today say, "That's so *basic*," they're essentially saying that whatever you just said or did was uncool, lame, pedestrian, and maybe even a little bit sad. So, let's say a student raised their hand and said I was too quiet during my presentation—which, for the record, was totally on purpose—I would then invite my students to discuss in pairs what that note might sound like as basic feedback versus positive and productive feedback, and then have them share their examples with the rest of the class.

My favorite aha moments as a teacher come when students realize they can say the same thing in different, more positive ways. Students don't want to be jerks or say things that will hurt a classmate's feelings—they usually just haven't been taught how to deliberately communicate with the intention of uplifting the other person. That's why it's important to explicitly teach your students how to tailor their feedback and always err on the positive and productive side before any creator in your class takes the stage.

Before students begin their projects, they first need to understand the characteristics and components of a high-quality presentation. Providing model presentations and online exemplars, such as the following, for students to evaluate with the presentation rubric featured in figure 3.1 (page 47) is a great way to clarify your expectations for students' work and what success looks like in this project.

- **Logan LaPlante: Hackschooling Makes Me Happy (https://youtu.be/h11u3vtcpaY):** I love using this talk as a model because when this thirteen-year-old presenter is asked the old question, "What do you want to be when you grow up?" his answer is simple: "*Happy!*" He then lays out his vision for an education system based on the study and practice of being happy and healthy. This talk beautifully captures everything I'm looking for in my students' presentations *and* my own professional life.

- **Mark Ronson: How Sampling Transformed Music (www.ted.com/talks/mark_ronson_how_sampling_transformed_music):** World-famous music producer Mark Ronson opens this TED Talk by demonstrating the very thing he's there to discuss: sampling music and making it your own. I encourage my students to do the same, especially when presenting about an activity or artform they are personally passionate about—create a space with instruments, artifacts, and so on, where others can engage with your idea or message. Plus, my students love seeing that even a celebrity like Mark Ronson can look a little awkward and humble on stage in front of a room full of brilliant people.

- **Josh Gad: Original Oratory Champion, Nationals 1998 (https://youtu.be/It1zvf_4JPE):** This talk is not a digital presentation; it has no slides and features one young man (who grew up to become Olaf in the Pixar movie *Frozen*) equipped with only his voice, gestures, and magnetic charm. I find that creating presentations is relatively easy for students because it's a skill that builds on what they've already learned as writers. Presenting, on the other hand, is more difficult to do well, and students benefit from watching a master at work. The video quality isn't great because this recording—like so many of us—comes from the late 1990s, but Josh Gad's hilarious and animated performance is a masterclass on how to grab hold of an audience and take them where they need to go.

## The Project

In this project, your young creators will design a presentation, deliver it in front of their peers, and post it online. This digital project is incredibly polarizing within a class—some students love it, some hate it, and some run straight out the door the minute they hear they'll be speaking in front of the class. However, in this information era, it is vital for students to overcome their fears and learn how to create presentations that clearly and concisely capture accurate and engaging content for both in-person and online audiences.

Figure 3.3 (page 50) outlines the steps a student in my class follows to successfully complete this digital project.

| **Presenter:** | **Presentation Title:** | **Date:** |
|---|---|---|
| **Prewrite** Step 1: Brainstorm ideas and select a topic of interest. Topic: _____ Step 2: Research information, multimedia, and interesting facts related to the topic. | | |
| **Draft** Step 3: Outline the presentation. Step 4: Type a draft script for the presentation and create draft slides. | | |
| **Rehearse and Revise** Step 5: Rehearse the presentation and score yourself with the rubric. Revise as needed. Step 6: Have at least two critical friends score the rehearsal with the rubric and fill out a Critical Friend Feedback Form. Revise as needed. Step 7: Rehearse with the teacher. Revise as needed. | | |
| **Proofread** Step 8: Edit the slides and script, correcting any errors in writing conventions and technical design. | | |
| **Publish** Step 9: Present to the class and record the presentation (live or webinar). Step 10: Publish the presentation online and complete an After-Project Reflection. | | |

**FIGURE 3.3:** *Presentation planning.*

*Visit **go.SolutionTree.com/technology** for a free reproducible version of this figure.*

Do you already have students create presentations using digital tools in your classroom, have a system that works well for you, and you're just here to learn more about sharing your students' work online? In that case, skip to the "Publish" section (page 57) of this project and begin reading at step 9. If you're new to this digital project, just know that it follows the five stages of the writing process for blog posts, essays, and most other written assignments: (1) prewrite, (2) draft, (3) revise, (4) proofread, and (5) publish. The only difference is that students prepare a script and slides for this project and rehearse their live or recorded presentations as they revise both.

## Prewrite

Prewriting is an essential preliminary step for students when preparing presentations. During this time, your creators explore possible topics worth covering and conduct research for relevant information and images. You should also show your students as many excellent models of public speaking as possible so they can visualize what it generally ought to look like when they take the stage. Prewriting allows presenters to identify their key points, curate visual aids, and begin crafting content with enthusiasm and purpose.

### Step 1: Brainstorm Ideas and Select a Topic of Interest

Students begin this project by brainstorming topics and selecting an area of focus. Perhaps you already have writing prompts, discussion material, and grade-level or content-specific questions that would make great topics for your students' presentations. That's awesome! I certainly love it when students present on topics related to our sixth-grade science or social studies standards, such as examining the Olmec Empire or comparing the impacts of the greenhouse effect on different ecosystems. However, I also use the Utah English language arts standards cited in chapter 1 (page 13) to empower my students to choose topics they are personally interested in for their digital presentations. Professional speakers aren't assigned topics—they bring what they know and love onstage with them, and so should students.

I provide each student with the presentation topic selection page shown in figure 3.4 to help my creators select topics that matter to them.

---

**Brainstorm**

1. What topic would you be most excited to explore in your presentation? Explain why.



2. What message would you like to explore and communicate in your presentation?



3. Who would be the intended audience for your presentation? Explain why.



4. What would be your purpose in creating this presentation (to inform, raise awareness, or create change)? How would you achieve that purpose?

---

**FIGURE 3.4:** *Student presentation topic selection.*

If students get stuck selecting topics for their presentations, I always give them one piece of advice: think local. If their idea is too big and broad—for example, homelessness—thinking local means considering community impacts, implications, and solutions. Thinking local means considering questions like, What does homelessness look like in our neighborhood? How does homelessness impact the students in our school? On the other hand, if their topic is too narrowly focused—for instance, one person they personally know who is without a house—encourage them to reflect that local interest outward to the world: How can the experiences of this one person help us better meet the needs of all people without houses in our city, state, or country? No matter what topics your students select, the connections to your community and to their daily lives should be apparent in every presentation.

### Step 2: Research Information, Multimedia, and Interesting Facts Related to the Topic

Once your students select their presentation topic, it's time for them to start researching. Of course, this will look different depending on your students' grade level, the content you teach, and the availability of books and online research tools you have in your classroom.

Chapter 1 (page 13) provides resources and lesson ideas for teaching media literacy and finding credible, reliable sources. I have my students do all their research online for this project because they can copy the links of articles and websites they use into a word processor document and later embed them directly into their presentations, saving them the trouble of going back and locating their sources' bibliographic information.

Students always ask, "How much research do I need to do?" Here's my answer: If you have five fascinating facts in your presentation—five compelling pieces of information you can share with your audience that makes them say, "Wow, that's super interesting"—then high-five, you're crushing the research game. Before students can outline their presentations, they must show me their "Five Fascinating Facts" form (figure 3.5, and page 156 in the appendix) so I can confirm that they are indeed fascinating and relevant to their presentation.

**Five Fascinating Facts**

Now that you have chosen a topic, it is time to do your research and find information to present to your audience. You may use books and other texts, along with online research tools, to find the five most fascinating facts that relate to your topic. Don't forget to cite your sources.

| Fact | Source |
| --- | --- |
| 1. | |
| 2. | |
| 3. | |
| 4. | |
| 5. | |

**FIGURE 3.5:** *Five fascinating facts form.*

## Draft

During the drafting phase, students flesh out their main points, experiment with different visual aids and presentation styles, and write scripts that capture the essential information they want to communicate in a tight, coherent structure. Drafting also allows students to remain flexible with their ideas, reconsider their position as they integrate new insights and information, and make necessary adjustments to enhance the clarity and impact of their messaging. As with writing blog posts, by encouraging young creators to embrace the drafting process, you are helping them design content that will captivate and inspire their audience.

### Step 3: Outline the Presentation

As described in chapter 1 (page 13), create a digital folder for every project in your class's shared drive. Within that folder, create a folder for each student to house all their resources and work. For this project, provide your creators with a PowerPoint template that includes the following slides.

- Title
- Introduction (introduce new idea or message)
- Fascinating Fact 1 and Insight (connect information to new idea or message)
- Fascinating Fact 2 and Insight (connect information to new idea or message)
- Fascinating Fact 3 and Insight (connect information to new idea or message)
- Fascinating Fact 4 and Insight (connect information to new idea or message)
- Fascinating Fact 5 and Insight (connect information to new idea or message)
- Conclusion (reiterate new idea or message)

The presentation outline shown in figure 3.6 (page 54) mirrors this design and includes sections outlining the content covered on each slide. I only give students the go-ahead to begin working on their slides once I have reviewed their completed outline.

This outline is incredibly structured and prescriptive and is intended as a starting place for students to organize their research and connect each piece back to their presentation's main idea. As students draft their scripts and slides, I encourage them to consolidate facts that belong together, group information thematically, and shift these pieces to create a natural flow of information throughout their presentation. Each creator's final presentation is uniquely designed according to that student's tastes and style.

There are three questions worth asking while reviewing a student's outline.

1. Is their idea or message engaging and original?
2. Have they made logical and compelling connections between their five fascinating facts and their idea or message?
3. Are they elaborating on each fascinating fact with an interesting insight?

When the answer to each question is *yes*, then students can move to the next step.

### Step 4: Type a Draft Script For the Presentation and Create Draft Slides

A chicken versus egg thing happens once students' outlines are finished: which comes first, the script or the slides? Let your students decide for themselves. Some will dive right into the script,

| **Presenter:** | **Presentation Title:** | **Date:** |
|---|---|---|
| **Introduction:** Strong hook, and then talk about your idea or your message. | | |
| **Fascinating Fact 1 and Insight:** How does your first fact connect to your idea or message? | | |
| **Fascinating Fact 2 and Insight:** How does your second fact connect to your idea or message? | | |
| **Fascinating Fact 3 and Insight:** How does your third fact connect to your idea or message? | | |
| **Fascinating Fact 4 and Insight:** How does your fourth fact connect to your idea or message? | | |
| **Fascinating Fact 5 and Insight:** How does your fifth fact connect to your idea or message? | | |
| **Conclusion:** Remind us of your idea or message and finish strong with a powerful closing thought. | | |

***FIGURE 3.6:*** *Presentation outline.*

drafting a fleshed-out version of their outline. Others will immediately open PowerPoint and start designing their presentations, populating slides with images they found during their research.

As a facilitator of their learning, try to give your students the necessary time and space to create without interference. Simply ensure they know you're always available to support them whenever needed. If they are all fully invested in steps 1–3, this stage of the process is about young creators discovering treasures along the paths they've created for themselves.

### Rehearse and Revise

During the rehearse and revise stage, creators leverage feedback from trusted friends and you—their coach and mentor—to refine their language and polish their delivery. Providing ample rehearsal time allows students to become more comfortable with their material, reducing anxiety and trepidation for nervous presenters. By carefully monitoring your students throughout this process, you will know when a student is ready to move on or when they need to keep practicing.

#### Step 5: Rehearse, Self-Score the Presentation With the Rubric, and Revise

Once students have completed drafts of *both* their slides and scripts, they are ready to begin rehearsing their presentations. It's important to hold off on providing them with too much feedback until now because many revisions that need to be made depend on performance. It's not about how the slides look or how the words read on the page; instead, it's about how they sound or look when performed for an audience.

When a student tells me they're done with their draft script and presentation, I hand them the rubric featured in figure 3.1 (page 47), help them find a quiet place to rehearse, and tell them to evaluate their own performance as it stands at that moment. My students' favorite place to rehearse alone is in our rather spacious sixth-grade storage closet—use the space within your classroom and its surrounding area to your advantage. In most school contexts, students sitting alone in the hall outside the door will be just fine. These early rehearsals typically look like students quietly whisper-reading their scripts aloud to themselves, which obviously doesn't help them self-evaluate their own physicality or voice as performers. This is OK; the point of these initial revisions and rehearsals is to make sure your creators are confident enough in their content, conventions, and designs to present to their critical friends.

#### Step 6: Peer Review the Rehearsal With the Rubric and Revise Based on Feedback

Once they're ready, your creators perform their presentations for at least two critical friends, who each score the presentation with the rubric and fill out the "Critical Friend Feedback Form" (page 157 in the appendix). These presentation run-throughs are like public previews of theatrical productions that take place prior to the show's official opening. Theatrical previews allow the creative team to identify problem areas and opportunities for improvements or adjustments in their production, and the same is true for students presenting for their critical friends. The goal is for students to support one another as creatives and improve their presentations with targeted feedback. It helps to remind students that, despite *all* the work they've already done, their presentations are works in progress until they are recorded and published. They should take every opportunity to make them that much better.

This is also the step where students who struggle with anxiety (or abject terror) about public speaking let themselves be known. Indeed, some students will flat-out refuse to present in front of anyone, let alone the whole class. I see this as an opportunity to help them work through and overcome their fears in the safest possible environment—their classroom. Take the time to research and talk with your students about how avoidance reinforces a phobia and how to overcome this (Moody, 2016). If this doesn't alleviate the fear, give them the option of delivering their final presentation to only you and the same two trusted peers they choose as their critical friends. It's important to understand that students' fears may come from factors outside the classroom and your scope of influence may be limited.

Here are three activities you can do with your students to help them overcome their fear of public speaking:

1. **Role-play exercises:** Engage students in role-play exercises where they can practice speaking in different situations (readers theater, mock debates, and so on).
2. **Toastmasters approach:** Implement a Toastmasters-like approach in the classroom, where students can practice short speeches (a single paragraph) on topics they are interested in.
3. **Breathing and relaxation techniques:** Teach students deep-breathing exercises and relaxation techniques to help manage anxiety before and during speaking. These techniques can help them calm their nerves and feel more confident.

### Step 7: Rehearse With the Teacher and Revise

I constantly watch my students rehearse, check in with anyone who's struggling, and offer small pieces of feedback throughout the entire creative process. However, I love this step because this is when I sit back and enjoy my young creators' presentations one at a time. As you meet with students, take notes on a rubric and talk through those notes as soon as they're done presenting. Like every other critical friend, share with them what you liked about their presentation, what you wonder about, and what you suggest moving forward. While I would love to linger in each of these conferences, I know I can't take longer than ten minutes with each student if I want to stand a reasonable chance of getting through them all.

## Proofread

Proofreading shouldn't take long at all given the amount of attention and feedback your students' presentations have already received up to this point. However, it is critical that your creators catch any glaring errors in their slides or scripts because mistakes, even small ones, are distracting for audiences and will diminish their work's overall impact.

### Step 8: Edit the Slides and Script, Correcting Any Errors

After conferencing, each writer carefully proofreads their presentations, making sure they haven't missed any glaring grammatical or technical errors on their slides. They also check one last time to make sure the transitions, animations, and other design elements they have included are working exactly as intended and don't interrupt the presentation's flow.

Every student's final step is to copy and paste their script piece by piece from their document into the notes section of each corresponding slide in their presentation. When students present to the class, they hold their script (as a single sheet or cut and pasted onto note cards). When they record their presentations, creators may do so as a webinar; for that, they'll need their scripts on the screen so they're not constantly looking down at a piece of paper and back up at the camera. Avoid letting your creators copy and paste their scripts into their presentations before this step, because if they need to make changes to their script, they will have to do it twice—in their document *and* presentation. Waiting until they have a final script saves the hassle of tracking changes across multiple programs.

## Publish

Unlike the other projects in this book, the final stage in this process comes in two parts: performance and publication. Like a standup comedian filming a performance and then releasing it as a Netflix special, your creators must deliver their presentations with both a live and online audience in mind. Thankfully, if they have fully committed to this process, they should be well-prepared to give an outstanding presentation.

### Step 9: Present to The Class and Record the Presentation

At last, it's time for students to take the stage and share what they've learned with the rest of the class. You might ask, when is that time? Is it one long day of presentations or several class sessions back to back? Well, that depends on what feels best to you and the structure of your class or school day.

In my class, I don't assign my creators a deadline for this digital project, so their completion typically mirrors a bell curve—a few students finish ahead of the pack, most finish within a week or two after that, and a handful lag behind the rest. When a student tells me they are finished proofreading their presentation, they present the next day. I love to start our mornings with these presentations, which usually take about five minutes to deliver. I pass out a rubric to every student in class, and they all turn in a score with notes for the presenter to reflect on following their performance.

As I described in this project's introduction, after a student presents, I invite the other creators in the room to share their positive and productive feedback with each other, first in pairs and then with the class. The first few creators who present set the bar for everyone else, and the verbal feedback they receive establishes what each class values most in presentations. As students share their feedback with each other, it is important for you to listen for comments you'll want everyone to hear and incorporate into their projects. Here are a few example comments I've spotlighted in the past.

- "I like how _____ looked like he was leaning into the audience the whole time, not folding down into the paper or turning at an angle away from us."
- "_____'s images were so perfect, it felt like her presentation was a picture book. I could have understood her message even if she hadn't said a word!"
- "After watching _____ present, I know I need to practice reading my script out loud more so my presentation is smoother and I don't have to look down so much."

I ask for volunteers to share once I bring everyone back together; if the creators who had the most useful feedback don't raise their hands, I "volun-tell" them to share their brilliant insights with the class.

In most classes, students present and receive feedback and a grade—that's it. That's the end of the story. That *kills* me! Students spend all this time perfecting these projects, and they should come away with more than a crinkled script and a handful of slides. That's why we record our presentations—to keep a record of their work that lives on long after their performance has ended. In addition to being able to share their presentations with family and friends, recorded presentations are the best teaching tool I have found for improving my students' practices as presenters. Classmate feedback is great, but nothing is more transformative for a young presenter than rewatching and analyzing their own performance like a professional athlete going over game tape, especially when they can analyze it with you, their coach. Students have two options for recording their presentations—live performance or webinar.

- **Live performance:** If a student opts to record their performance live in front of the class, I assign two students to film them on two different cameras (one with my phone, the other with a DSLR camera) on either side of the speaker at roughly 45-degree angles. Scan the QR code in the "Creators at Work" section of this chapter (page 45) to see what these angles look like for the viewer. My creators learn the fundamentals of filmmaking during film school as described in chapter 5 (page 77), so the students who film these presentations know how to frame their shots, consider composition as needed, and follow the speaker like Steadicam operators. The speaker is also mic'd up, and a sound mixer is recording their audio on my laptop. Following their presentation, I drop the presenter's video and audio files into their digital folder, and they can edit the video together in whatever way feels best to them. Some go all out, adding music and slides and cutting back and forth between cameras; others just turn in my phone's recording and call it a day. Either is great, and it's entirely up to them.
- **Webinar:** The other option, now available to my post-pandemic creators, is to record their presentations in PowerPoint or Zoom as a webinar—to compare options, revisit chapter 1 (page 13). While these recordings lack the life and energy only achievable with handheld video, I love this option because it's just so easy. Students sit down at their computer and click record in PowerPoint (or I can start a Zoom session), turn the camera on, hit record, launch their presentation, and begin. They can record on their own at any time, and we just drop the recording in their digital folder when they finish. That's it! They're done . . . Well, almost.

### Step 10: Publish the Presentation Online and Complete an After-Project Reflection

The moment a student posts their presentation recording online—either on their own website or on one of our class's platforms—they always let out a big sigh of relief. After all the time spent brainstorming, outlining, drafting, and rehearsing, they are finally *done*. Well, except for the critically important step of completing the "After-Project Reflection Form" (page 158 in the appendix) to examine what they liked about their own work, what they could have improved, and what they will do differently going forward.

Now, they're done.

. . . . . . . . . . . . . . . . . . . . . . . . . . . . . . . . . . . . . . . . . . . . . . . . .

## Conclusion

Let's check back in with this project's objective: *I will empower my students' voices by teaching them to share thoughtfully crafted presentations with an online audience of viewers.* You and your creators worked through this process step-by-step because their ideas and messages have value and need to reach as many people as possible. Here are three variations on this project that are easier to implement and, once posted online, achieve the same objective.

- **Slideshow:** Your creators can record their audio in PowerPoint and publish their slideshow as interactive content for their websites or post it on the internet as a video file.
- **Publish presentations:** Students can post their presentation only, without video, and include their script in the notes section of each slide so online readers have access to both.
- **Original oration:** Presenters can use a teleprompter app on a tablet or phone to record themselves performing their scripts as a monologue without their slides and then post the video online.

# CHAPTER 4
# Podcasts

**PROJECT OBJECTIVE**

I will empower my students' voices by teaching them to share information, raise awareness, and advocate for positive change through podcasts.

### Definition of *Podcast*

**noun**
A digital audio file made available on the internet for downloading to a computer or mobile device, typically available as a series, new installments of which can be received by subscribers automatically.

**verb**
Make (a digital audio file) available as a podcast.

—*Oxford English Dictionary Online*

## CREATORS AT WORK

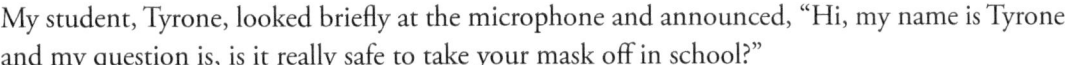

My student, Tyrone, looked briefly at the microphone and announced, "Hi, my name is Tyrone, and my question is, is it really safe to take your mask off in school?"

This is a story that began in the spring of 2022; cases of COVID-19 were steadily declining in Salt Lake City, and students began asking me, "Is it safe to take off our masks?" Honestly, I didn't know, or at least I wasn't sure enough about my answer to risk getting it wrong. Luckily, at that same time, I received an email from my friend Ali Vallarta, the incredible host of *City Cast Salt Lake*, which is part of a network of one-of-a-kind podcasts produced in cities around the United States. Ali wanted my students to help produce an episode of her podcast by writing and recording questions about a topic of their choosing with her present at the school. Then, she would get the answers from an expert guest on her show. I thought it would be amazing if I could get answers for all my students' COVID-19 questions from Dr. Angela Dunn, state epidemiologist for the Utah Department of Health throughout most of the pandemic.

Ali listened to Tyrone speak and replied, "I love how you read that, Tyrone, but you have to lean a little closer to the mic."

Tyrone sat up in his chair, leaned closer to the mic, and tried again. This time, Ali gave him a big thumbs-up. "Perfect! Now, try the next question."

While Ali recorded each student one at a time across the hall, a handful of students and I reviewed our remaining questions. First, we wanted to eliminate any easy questions we could answer ourselves to maximize our time on the show with Dr. Dunn. We had previously participated in a wonderful discussion about the qualities of a *great* question, and because the students knew their questions were going to be evaluated by a professional (in Ali Vallarta), posed to an expert (Dr. Dunn), and listened to by a real audience (including families and friends), they took this task very seriously.

Sergio held up his paper and pointed at a question like he was poking it in the chest. "I think we should change this question: 'Why did you become a doctor?' It's too . . . basic."

Another student, Daniela, agreed. "We shouldn't ask her why she became a doctor—that doesn't have anything to do with COVID, which is what our whole episode is about. We should ask her what it was like being a doctor during COVID!"

Most of my writers liked the idea, but Sergio still wasn't convinced. "Yeah, but on the podcast rubric (see figure 4.1), it says our question is supposed to draw out compelling answers. And, I don't know, I feel like there's gotta be a more compelling question than just, what was it like, right?"

"Like what?" I asked.

Sergio thought about it. "You know she's going to say it was all really hard. So maybe, like, did she ever want to quit?"

Daniela sat up taller. "Oh! What about, have you had second thoughts about being a doctor?"

The other writers totally loved it. Sergio even gave Daniela a high five, then immediately headed for the hand sanitizer. Ali popped her head into the room. "Who's next?"

Daniela said, "Sergio is. He's got a *great* question for Dr. Dunn!"

Teachers often feel like they need to have all the answers for their students. In those moments, we need to remember that our job isn't to answer all our students' questions—our job is to teach students how to access the accurate, factual answers necessary to take informed action in their lives. "Is it safe to take off our masks?" I could have answered their question, and what a missed opportunity that would have been.

**DUE IN PART TO** the pandemic, some media analysts have begun referring to the pandemic era as the golden age of podcasts (McCarron & Yamanaka, 2022). Podcasting refers to the creation and serial distribution of online audio files directly to consumers' media devices for listening at home or on the go via streaming or downloaded media files. Combining the powers of storytelling, conversations, true-crime obsessions, and ease of use, podcasting's impact as an auditory form of digital media consumption is remarkable in a world that relies so heavily on visual stimuli (Nelson, 2021).

Podcasts can be informational or narrative—rooted in reality or your students' imaginations. Your creators can produce podcasts on any topic and tell any story as part of a series or a one-off episode, so long as they balance their recorded voices with other sounds—music, sound effects, background noises, and so on. The most common types of podcasts include the interview, solo or monologue, news, panel, nonfiction storytelling, and fictional storytelling. You can even design your class project as a StudyCast, a podcast recording intended solely for classroom use and not distributed to the general public (Cain, Cain, & Daigle, 2021). Students can make StudyCasts to help them learn more about a topic or demonstrate their mastery of a concept, supporting both engagement and content retention.

|  | **3** | **2** | **1** |
|---|---|---|---|
| **Storytelling and Structure** | The podcast shares an interesting story or message that moves the audience's thoughts or actions.<br><br>The podcast has an excellent hook that engages the audience.<br><br>The podcast has a clear beginning, middle, and end. | The podcast tells a story or communicates a message to the audience.<br><br>The podcast has a good hook that engages the audience.<br><br>The podcast has some sense of a beginning, middle, and end. | The podcast's story or message is unclear.<br><br>The podcast does not have a hook that engages the audience.<br><br>The podcast lacks an organized structure. |
| **Research and Interviews** | Quantitative and qualitative information thoughtfully supports the story or message of the podcast.<br><br>High-quality interview questions draw compelling answers that add to the podcast's story or message. | Quantitative and qualitative information is present in the podcast.<br><br>Good questions are answered by the interview subject or subjects. | Little to no quantitative or qualitative information is present in the podcast.<br><br>Interview or interviews do not add much to the podcast's story or message. |
| **Presentation:**<br>**Voice**<br>**Volume**<br>**Tone**<br>**Modulation**<br>**Energy**<br>**Enthusiasm** | Student engages the audience with a confident and dynamic speaking style.<br><br>Student speaks clearly and enunciates throughout. | Student engages the audience with an adequate speaking style, but occasional hesitations or lack of confidence are noticeable.<br><br>Student speaks somewhat clearly and enunciates at times. | Student struggles to engage the audience because of weak speaking style, hesitations, lack of confidence, or monotone delivery.<br><br>Student's speech is muffled and difficult to understand. |
| **Audio** | Podcast has high-quality interview audio. Narrations are clear and easy to understand.<br><br>Score or additional audio enhance the listening experience and draw the audience into the podcast. | Interview audio and narrations can be heard and understood by the audience.<br><br>Score or additional audio are used to enhance the podcast. | Audio recordings are low-quality and distracting.<br><br>Score or additional audio detract from the podcast. |
| **Editing** | Deliberate editing decisions move the podcast forward from beginning to end.<br><br>Podcast features seamless integration of transitions, audio effects, and thoughtful cuts. | Some editing decisions help move the podcast along.<br><br>Podcast features transitions, audio effects, and cuts. | Poor editing leaves the podcast feeling slow or hard to understand.<br><br>Podcast features little to no use of transitions, audio effects, or cuts. |

**FIGURE 4.1:** *Podcast rubric.*

*Visit* **go.SolutionTree.com/instruction** *for a free reproducible version of this figure.*

Before students begin their projects, they first need to understand the characteristics and components of a well-produced podcast. Providing model podcasts for students to evaluate with the podcast rubric shown in figure 4.1 (page 63) is a great way to clarify expectations for students' productions and what success can sound like on this project.

- **Gen Z Media (GZM) Classroom (www.gzmclassroom.com):** This is my top pick for podcasts and educator resources. The GZM site has an array of fiction and nonfiction podcasts to choose from, as well as classroom tools like listening guides, digital explore and choice boards, and videos telling you how to use them. I relied on the show *Podcast Title Pending*—yes, that's its title—for advice when I started podcasting with my students, and the show "Six_Minutes" is everyone's favorite serial adventure story. They even record an entire show in Spanish, "Seis_Minutos."
- **One Voice Youth Choir (www.onevoicechildren.org/podcast):** One Voice Youth Choir's mission is to inspire the world through the power of children's voices. Composed of Utah children ages 5–18, they have more than four million subscribers on YouTube and have carried the call to empower young voices on tour with them all over the world. They now also offer *Finding Our Voice: The One Voice Children Podcast*, on which members of the choir write, edit, record, and host episodes with topics ranging from hot trends and body images to honoring diverse cultures.
- ***Inherited* (https://yr.media/inherited):** *Inherited* is a climate storytelling podcast by, for, and about young people. In a study by Hickman and colleagues, 59 percent of young people reported being very or extremely worried about climate change, and more than 45 percent of respondents said their feelings about climate change negatively affected their daily life and functioning (Hickman et al., 2021). Against this backdrop and produced by Youth Radio Media, *Inherited* features sound-rich stories created by youth committed to addressing this crisis by raising awareness and sharing the experiences of communities and individuals whose lives have been directly impacted by the changing climate.

## The Project

In this digital project, students will form teams with assigned roles to collaboratively create a podcast episode. Figure 4.2 outlines the steps students in my class follow to successfully complete their podcast. There are three stages of podcast production: (1) preproduction, (2) production, and (3) postproduction. Throughout this project, podcast teams will progress through these stages at their own pace. While you'll want to teach whole-group lessons on script writing, audio recording, editing, and so on, you will also want to allot time during class and outside of school hours for students to work on their podcasts wherever they are in the process.

For this project, I present each step as if students are creating an interview-style podcast episode with at least one guest. This is the most common type of podcast format I've seen used across classroom settings and age groups, and it leads perfectly into the short film documentary project featured in chapter 6 (page 105). However, your students can use these same skills to produce whatever type of podcast appeals to them most.

| **Podcasters:** | **Title and topic of podcast episode:** |
|---|---|
| **Preproduction** <br> Step 1: Brainstorm ideas for the podcast and select a topic or subject. <br> Topic/Subject: _____ <br> Step 2: Write a treatment for the podcast and pitch the project. <br> Step 3: Research information and interesting facts to include in the podcast. <br> Step 4: Draft interview questions for the podcast. | |
| **Production** <br> Step 5: Conduct interviews. <br> Step 6: Script and record narration along with additional audio. | |
| **Postproduction** <br> Step 7: Edit the podcast: interviews, narration, music, transitions, and sound effects. <br> Step 8: Play the rough cut for the teacher and at least two critical friends. We will each give you a score with the rubric and a Critical Friend Feedback Form. Continue editing as needed. <br> Step 9: Present the final product during the podcast listening party. <br> Step 10: Publish the podcast online and complete an After-Project Reflection. | |

**FIGURE 4.2:** *Podcast planning.*

*Visit **go.SolutionTree.com/technology** for a free reproducible version of this figure.*

## *Preproduction*

During preproduction, each podcasting team will decide together what they want their episode to be about and complete the subsequent steps to begin production. To facilitate the successful completion of all preproduction tasks and ensure a fair distribution of work among team members, I require my podcast teams to assign each of these individual tasks to one or two students.

- Write the treatment.
- Pitch the podcast.
- Conduct research.
- Draft interview questions.

Teams are ready to begin the preproduction process once they have assigned these tasks strategically and fairly to their members.

### *Step 1: Brainstorm Ideas for the Podcast and Select a Topic*

During the first lesson, you'll want to listen to at least two model podcast episodes that your students can evaluate using their rubrics. In my class, we listen to the first two episodes of *Podcast Title Pending* from GZM Media, which is listed in the "Project" section. This podcast is perfect for this lesson because it's about making a podcast from concept to publication and marketing. Each episode is five minutes long and includes an interview with an expert guest, and all GZM's podcasts are made with young audiences in mind.

After finishing our discussion, students organize themselves into teams of four (if you need to have an odd number on a team, three is better than five) and begin brainstorming ideas for their own podcasts.

Interview podcasts typically either focus on a topic (such as a writers' workshop or the best hikes in the community) or a subject (such as a famous star with a new movie coming out). My students use the podcast topic selection page (see figure 4.3) to select a subject the whole team is interested in or a topic they want to investigate, elevate, or propose solutions for in their episode.

**Brainstorm**

1. What topic would you be most excited to explore in your podcast? Explain why.

2. Who would be the intended audience for your podcast? Explain why.

3. What themes would you like to explore and communicate in your podcast?

4. What would be your purpose in making this podcast (to inform others, raise awareness, or create change)? How would you achieve that purpose?

5. Who would you need to interview for your podcast, and what would you want to ask them?

**FIGURE 4.3:** Podcast topic selection.

Visit **go.SolutionTree.com/technology** *for a free reproducible version of this figure.*

Teams might want to interview a structural engineer about the various calculations they complete in a single day, and another team might do a deep dive into the differences between conduction and convection. Students also discuss who their target audience should be, the themes they would want to explore and communicate, and their purpose in making the episode (inform others, create change, and so on).

### Step 2: Write a Treatment for the Podcast and Pitch the Project

A podcast treatment is a written summary that hosts and producers use to outline their episodes and present them to others to raise support for their program. In addition to the topic, audience, theme, and purpose, the podcast treatment (see figure 4.4) includes spaces for students to write a logline (one line that sums up your episode for listeners) and basic story arc for their interview (Act 1, Act 2, and Act 3).

| Recording Team: | Logline: |
|---|---|
| Topic: | Act 1: |
| Audience: | Act 2: |
| Theme (message): | Act 3: |

**FIGURE 4.4:** *Podcast treatment.*

*Visit **go.SolutionTree.com/technology** for a free reproducible version of this figure.*

At this point, some students will say they thought this was supposed to be an interview, not a story. That is correct. While every interview takes unexpected turns, every great interviewer writes questions for their guests with a clear beginning, middle, and end in mind for their conversation—just like a good story. They may not know the answers to their questions yet, but they know the direction their questions should take them and where that place is in relation to where the interview starts. In Act 1, students should draft their first question to be an excellent launching point for their conversation. In Act 2, it's helpful to list a couple more questions that signal where the team intends to center the interview. Act 3 serves as the opportunity for a final question that captures the team's main idea, theme, and the point they want to make with their episode.

If students say they're still confused, just ask them, "Have you ever wanted something from your parents, but you knew that coming right out and asking for it wouldn't get you where you wanted to go? So, you came up with questions or conversation pieces that started somewhere else and then steadily made your way toward asking for the thing you wanted all along. Well, that's what I mean when I say you'll write a story arc for your interview!"

Once their treatment is complete, each team selects one spokesperson to pitch their podcast concept to me. During these five-minute sessions, I like to ask the whole team quick, probing questions to clarify any confusion I might have and determine how interested everyone really is in the topic or subject they've chosen. Afterward, I fill out the "Critical Friend Feedback Form" (page 157 in the appendix), letting them know what I liked about their podcast pitch, what I still wonder about, and one suggestion I have for the group. Sometimes, I invite guests like our school's librarian or media specialist or local podcasters to conduct these pitching sessions with me, upping the ante for my presenting students and providing them with further feedback. If I determine their treatment needs more work, then the students go back and rework their concept; however, if a team has a solid concept they are clearly excited about, then their project gets the green light, and they move on to step 3.

### Step 3: Research Information and Interesting Facts to Include in the Podcast

The goal of the research process for students is to collect quantitative (measurable, numbers-based) and qualitative (categorical, language-based) data that underlies the importance and relevance of their podcasts and interviews. This research will be used to draft the podcast script and questions and inform editing decisions in postproduction. As students gather facts and figures in a digital document, make sure they also record the bibliographical information as they go so it's easy to cite their sources as needed in the episode. Revisit chapter 1 (page 13) for resources and lesson ideas for teaching media literacy to students and finding credible, reliable sources online.

As with previous projects in this book, have your students begin by finding five fascinating facts on their topic or subject (see the "Five Fascinating Facts Form" on page 156 in the appendix). Also, since so much of the information presented in a podcast comes from interviews conducted with a variety of individuals, it's critical that your podcasters use research to narrow their search for qualified and compelling interview subjects. Thanks to video conferencing platforms like Webex and Zoom, students could hypothetically interview guests from all around the world; however, I encourage my students to select individuals who are *local* and accessible for in-person interviews. They should look to their own communities for the expertise and experience needed to speak thoughtfully about relevant issues in their lives. Figure 4.5 shows the template I provide my students for their initial emails to potential interviewees.

> Hi [name],
>
> My name is [student name], and I am a sixth-grade student at Meadowlark Elementary. My classmates and I are producing a podcast episode about [topic], and we would like to interview you for our project. If you are willing to be interviewed by us, please contact our teacher at [email address] or [phone number].
>
> Sincerely,
>
> [Student name]

**FIGURE 4.5:** *Podcast interview request message.*

To ensure my students' safety, the initial email and all further communications are run through my email address and telephone number. The only exception to this rule is if the interview subject is a student's friend, family member, or trusted adult in our school community who they invite in person to be on their podcast. Even then, ensure students copy you on any subsequent emails and include you in any text conversations related to the project.

Once students know who they want to interview, they need their subject's permission to record their conversation. There are countless release forms to choose from online. My favorite interview release form is pictured in figure 4.6.

---

**INTERVIEW RELEASE FORM**

Project name: _____    Date: _____

Interviewer: _____    Tape number: _____

Name of person(s) interviewed: _____

Address: _____

Telephone number: _____    Date of birth: _____

Email address: _____

By signing the form below, you give your permission for any tapes and/or photographs made during this project to be used by researchers and the public for educational purposes, including publications, exhibitions, World Wide Web, and presentations. By giving your permission, you do not give up any copyright or performance rights that you may hold.

I agree to the uses of these materials described above, except for any restrictions noted below.

Name: _____    Date: _____
        *Please print*

Signature: _____

---

**FIGURE 4.6:** *Interview release form.*

*Visit **go.SolutionTree.com/technology** for a free reproducible version of this figure.*

### Step 4: Draft Interview Questions for the Podcast

The first rule of writing high-quality questions is to keep them open-ended. Nothing slows down an interview faster than asking a question with a simple yes-or-no answer. Thankfully, it's easy to transform a yes-or-no question into an open-ended one. For example, instead of asking, "Did you enjoy school today?" encourage students to ask, "What were some things you learned at school today?" Another way to avoid a one-word answer is to have students phrase questions that will elicit a thorough response, such as the following.

- "Tell me about . . ."
- "Explain why . . ."
- "How did you . . ."
- "Describe for us . . ."

Because our podcast episodes typically run five to ten minutes, I limit my podcasters to three to five well-written questions per interview subject, understanding that follow-up questions will likely flow naturally during their conversations. Each team turns in their written questions for review. I conference with students whose questions need to be revised, and after any necessary changes have been made, their questions are sent to the interviewees for final approval.

## Production

Before recording can begin, each student needs to choose a production role on their podcasting team. The most common jobs on a podcast team are as follows.

- **Host:** The host is the voice of the podcast who introduces each episode, guides discussions, interviews the guests, and thanks the audience at the end.
- **Producer:** The producer oversees the production process, manages logistics, and ensures everything runs smoothly.
- **Sound engineer:** The sound engineer handles the technical aspects of recording, such as setting up microphones and ensuring good audio quality.
- **Editor:** The editor is responsible for postproduction work, including editing audio clips, sound design, and ensuring the podcast sounds polished and professional.

Once students have picked their roles, they can finally begin recording. To do this, they'll need access to whatever audio recording equipment you have available. Remember, the only two *must-have* pieces of equipment each podcast team needs are a recording device (a computer, a tablet, even a smartphone) and a microphone for capturing and recording audio. Indeed, the comfort and ease of podcasting allow students to record wherever and as frequently as they want (Dversnes & Blikstad-Balas, 2023). However, remember that while you can get away with a host and interview subject passing a mic back and forth as they ask and answer questions, it's best if *everyone* who is speaking has their *own* mic. This, plus the improved audio quality, is why it's not necessary but very nice to have external mics for this project. Fortunately, USB microphones that plug right into student laptops can be purchased for less than twenty U.S. dollars each.

The greatest technical challenge in creating a student podcast prior to the pandemic was figuring out how to record multiple voices on the same audio recording platform; however, during remote learning, we all got used to using Zoom, which is now my students' go-to tool for recording interviews remotely and in person. Other programs like Audacity and Adobe Audition can also create separate audio tracks for each speaker on your podcast, and technology advances so quickly that there will likely be more options on the market by the time you read this. Run a quick search of what's out there and select the program that makes the most sense for you.

Because Zoom has become a commonplace tool since the start of the COVID-19 pandemic, I have included the following basic podcast recording instructions that (as of this writing) work with Zoom.

1. Before starting a meeting, log into the Zoom app and click Settings.
2. Click the Recording tab. Make sure you have selected Local Recording so the audio files will be saved on your computer.
3. Select Record a Separate Audio File of Each Participant. Now, when you record your interview or discussion, an audio file will be created for each individual logged into that meeting, even if they're sitting together in the same room but recording on separate devices. During postproduction, these individual audio tracks will make it easier for the editor to eliminate problematic noises, pauses, interruptions, and so on.
4. Launch the Zoom meeting. Ask all participants to adjust their audio levels to ensure they are recording at an appropriate volume.
5. Begin recording. Have each participant clap once loudly so the editor can easily sync all recordings by lining up the volume spike on all audio tracks.
6. When the interview is finished, stop the recording. Zoom will save all audio files to the host's device.

Throughout production, the sound engineer needs to listen for any noises that might distract or impede the audience from hearing the words being spoken. If possible, have each participant record in a quiet, tight space to eliminate echoes and natural reverb. Eliminate as much background noise as possible (such as air conditioners, fans and laptop fans, and machines that buzz or hum), use external mics whenever possible, and record thirty seconds of ambient sound to lay over any gaps in postproduction.

### Step 5: Conduct Interviews

People, including adults, often get nervous or tighten up once they're in front of a microphone, so interviewers need to ease their subjects into the conversation. I encourage my students to begin their interviews with factual, straightforward questions and save the more personal or emotionally loaded material for later in the interview when their subject has had time to get more comfortable. Students should always finish interviews by asking their subjects, "Is there anything else you want to say or anything we forgot to cover?" And, of course, no interview is ever complete until the interviewer thanks their guest for their time and participation.

Like adult podcasters, students are likely to come into their projects already knowing what they want to say and the point they want to make. Encourage your students to stay open to changing their minds or shifting their perspectives based on what they learn during their interviews. Also, remind your podcasters that they are creating this content in service to their audience, so when they're considering follow-up questions or continuing with a conversation, they should think about what the audience wants and needs to know most about their topic.

### Step 6: Script and Record Narration Along With Additional Audio

On other digital projects, your students would have drafted scripts during preproduction. However, podcasts are incredibly organic and unpredictable. Even if you know how an interview will go, you can't write the intro or outro for a conversation until after it's taken place. Students organize their intros and outros using the intro and outro organizer (see figure 4.7) to write their scripts and record their narrations, along with any additional audio they want for their episode, on their computer's audio recording software. If you don't have a dedicated audio recording and editing program on your computer, I recommend Audacity (free) or Adobe Audition (not free but includes some awesome features).

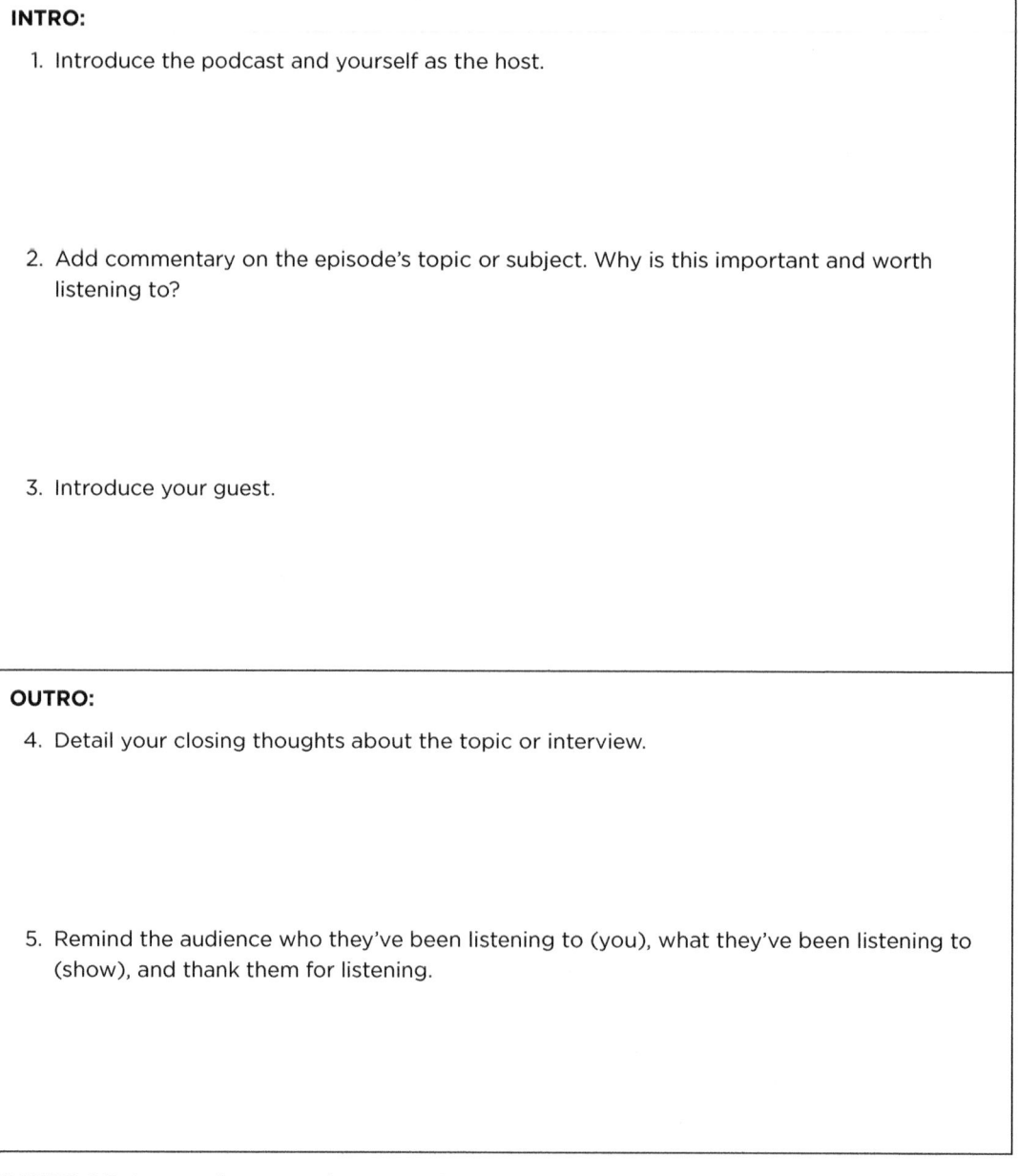

**INTRO:**
1. Introduce the podcast and yourself as the host.
2. Add commentary on the episode's topic or subject. Why is this important and worth listening to?
3. Introduce your guest.

**OUTRO:**
4. Detail your closing thoughts about the topic or interview.
5. Remind the audience who they've been listening to (you), what they've been listening to (show), and thank them for listening.

**FIGURE 4.7:** *Intro and outro podcast organizer.*
*Visit **go.SolutionTree.com/technology** for a free reproducible version of this figure.*

## Postproduction

Postproduction is the stage in which young creators edit, refine, and enhance their audio content before posting it online. During postproduction, students stitch together their episodes on editing software, add elements like music or sound effects, and eliminate any glitches or errors that may detract from the overall listening experience. Teams also solicit feedback on their rough cuts prior to publishing, ensuring a higher-quality product for their listeners to enjoy.

### Step 7: Edit the Podcast

You decide how much time you want your students to spend editing their podcasts, but they should be able to export the files for the intro, interview, and outro from their recording software into the editing software (if they're not the same program) and assemble those pieces in one forty-five-minute class session. Beyond that, there are different options editors can explore for making their podcast sound like it was produced by pros.

- **Music, sound effects, and transitions:** Add elements to make the episode more engaging and cohesive from beginning to end (check out the open-source music options in chapter 5, page 77).
- **Topping and tailing:** Trim the excess audio from the beginning and end of a recording.
- **Leveling:** Adjust the volume levels of the audio tracks to ensure consistent sound throughout the podcast.
- **Noise reduction:** Eliminate unwanted background noise.
- **Audio cleanup:** Remove distracting elements like coughs, pauses, dogs barking, and so on.

### Step 8: Play the Rough Cut for the Teacher and at Least Two Critical Friends

For this project, I suggest playing the rough cut of each podcast on your computer with two different podcast teams: (1) the team who created the episode and (2) another student podcast team to review it. Listen to the podcast together and then discuss it using the podcast rubric (figure 4.1, page 63) and the "Critical Friend Feedback Form" (page 157 in the appendix). This provides the podcasters with valuable feedback, and your team of reviewers goes back to work with greater insights and ideas for revising their own episodes.

### Step 9: Present the Final Product During the Podcast Listening Party

While many teachers assign due dates for projects, consider providing your film crews with a release date when they need to finish their podcasts to debut them at a podcast listening party.

This step is not a requirement, and you are welcome to completely disregard the rest of this paragraph. But after all the hard work you and your students put into this project, a public exhibition and celebration of their creative achievement is certainly deserved and always a hit. It can be as simple as an afternoon or evening exhibition for friends and families at school, where everyone wanders from station to station, listening to the different episodes and interacting with the creators. You can even combine this with an exhibition for any other digital projects your students completed throughout the year. No matter what, create fun, meaningful opportunities for your content creators to watch others enjoy their work.

### Step 10: Publish the Podcast Online and Complete an After-Project Reflection

Whether you're posting your students' podcasts on your school's learning management system or your class's preferred podcast hosting platform (review your options in chapter 1, page 13), you'll want to discuss with your podcast teams how broadly they want their work distributed and how they plan to reach their target audience. This is a team decision they must make together, and I always look forward to facilitating that conversation.

As always, before your digital content creators move on to their next project, have them reflect on their podcasting experience by completing an "After-Project Reflection Form" (page 158 in the appendix).

## Conclusion

Let's revisit our objective for this project: *I will empower my students' voices by teaching them to share information, raise awareness, and advocate for positive change through podcasts.* This project is all about teaching students to share with others the things they personally value or find interesting. If you still want your students creating digital projects that leverage audio recordings to accomplish that task but require less time and coordination than a podcast, here are a few related project ideas for your students to consider.

- Record a thirty- to sixty-second, audio-only public service announcement on your chosen topic, like an ad that might play before or after a popular podcast. This would provide students with preproduction, production, and postproduction experience but with a much simpler product and shorter timeline.

- Create a slideshow presentation on your topic with recorded audio playing over each slide. Students would still need to learn to record narration and edit their audio with other media elements to tell a compelling story, but they could complete this project independently without a team backing them up.

- Record an audio interview with an expert on your chosen topic. Students could still edit the audio if they want, but conducting an effective interview is perhaps the most valuable learning experience in this project. Cutting everything from the production besides the interview would focus all attention on this conversation's importance.

# PART II
# DIGITAL VIDEOS

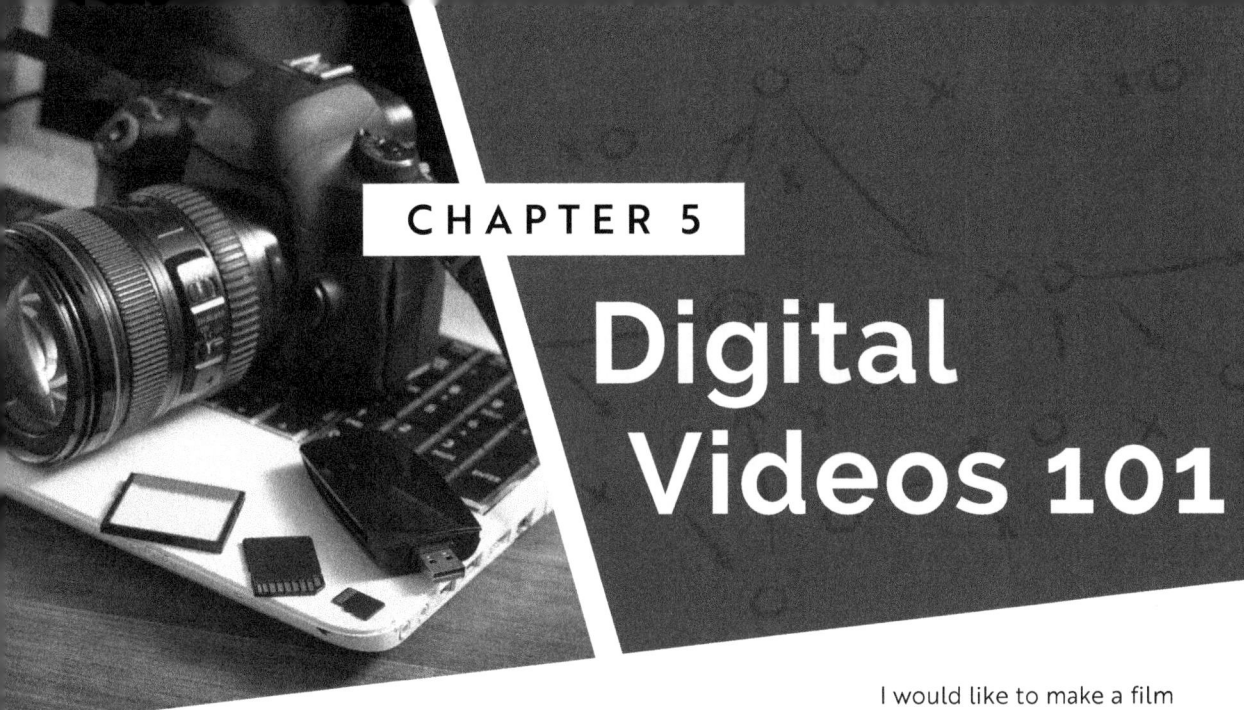

# CHAPTER 5

# Digital Videos 101

> I would like to make a film
> to tell children it's good to be alive.
>
> —Hayao Miyazaki

**IN PART I OF THIS BOOK,** I discussed digital projects that transform students into content creators sharing their written and recorded words with online audiences. Now, in part II, it's time to take their work to the next level by reframing these young authors as auteurs, expanding the skills they've developed to create original digital films in the classroom.

Teaching students how to produce high-quality videos in class has the power to elevate traditional writing projects and instructional practices by centering them within the media young people consume most. By incorporating visuals, audio, music, and other multimedia elements into a finished film product, your students will engage with their writing in a more dynamic and immersive way, fostering a deeper connection to the content they're producing.

Toddlers watch videos on tablets and TVs before they form sentences, which is why students inherently understand this art form and its approach to storytelling more naturally than they do the work we complete in class. While we must work hard to cultivate students' love for writing, they enter our classrooms already engaged in a long-term, loving relationship with videos and film. Rather than fighting that relationship, we should leverage it to equip our students with the skills necessary to navigate and excel in a media-driven world. This chapter shows you how by exploring the benefits of video production and the many aspects of the production process, as well as some ways to amplify your students' voices through online video sharing.

## The Benefits of Video Production

Whether they were projected on pull-down screens or big boxy televisions precariously mounted on walls, some of my favorite films were the ones I first watched in school as a student. Most importantly, screening films and short videos with students is an effective and useful classroom practice. No matter what you teach, viewing high-quality short films connected to your class's subject enhances memorization, comprehension, internalization of information, and creative thinking (Kabadayi, 2012). Films are powerful instructional vehicles for delivering content, conveying concepts, clarifying misconceptions, building students' empathy and awareness, reducing isolation, and creating emotional connections between students and subject matter (Blasco, Moreto, Blasco, Levites, & Janaudis, 2015). In particular, documentary filmmaking has a long tradition of drawing attention to stories and issues that are largely unknown to mainstream audiences, surfacing inequities and injustices for students who were previously unaware (Stille, 2011). Films are a powerful medium for fostering empathy and understanding among students as they delve into different perspectives, experiences, and information.

While watching a video can be a profound learning experience, nothing beats having students produce their own videos. Filmmaking provides students with innovative ways of telling a story, applying research skills, and investigating a topic while simultaneously strengthening students' technical and multimedia skills, preparing them to meet the demands of contemporary cultural and work environments (LePage & Courey, 2011). As a teacher of multilingual learners, I especially appreciate how filmmaking provides students with a visual means of expressing sophisticated thoughts that would be far more difficult to verbalize or write about in class. When you think of student-produced videos as visual essays, you realize they often surpass the complexity of meaning a student could produce through writing, and they empower students to make meaning and transmit their learning to others in exciting and intrinsically motivating ways (Meager, 2017).

The impact video production has on students' sense of agency and ownership has been demonstrated across academic settings and among diverse student populations. In India, for example, researchers gave ten- to twelve-year-olds video cameras and asked them to become observational filmmakers. They found that the children's ability to gain access to the physical spaces of street-side shops, as well as the visual and auditory social interactions captured on film, created opportunities for constructing new kinds of knowledge about the community and its residents (Meager, 2017). Not only did the children get to share the people and places they know and love, but the camera also gave them the authority to be close to a scene where they might otherwise have been seen as a nuisance and shooed away.

Documentary filmmaking is also used as a reverse-inclusion strategy to help students on the autism spectrum develop social skills (LePage & Courey, 2011). Equipped with user-friendly computers, cameras, lighting, and microphones, students at the Autism Social Connection in San Francisco record interviews with typically developing peers about behaviors and social norms, and then they reenact what they determine to be sociable behavior on film (LePage & Courey, 2011). This type of video modeling is especially effective for individuals with autism because it is highly motivating and engaging, it focuses attention directly on targeted actions or cues, and it relieves anxiety by removing individuals from the intensity and uncertainty of spontaneous social interactions (Charlop-Christy, Le, & Freeman, 2001).

In all these contexts, video production exists as a collaborative art form. As part of a film crew, students take on roles according to their interests, collaborate as a team to solve problems, and craft a finished product to showcase for fellow students, teachers, and parents. The notions of group work, taking responsibility, fulfilling obligations, and experiencing collective achievement are all developed through filmmaking (Kabadayi, 2012). These digital projects are also ideal for service learning and civic engagement; for example, short films can amplify the work of community groups, advance schoolwide initiatives, or tell the stories of everyday heroes, just to name a few.

The increasing availability of digital tools at our fingertips, along with the rapid growth of video sharing and social media platforms, has all but removed technology as a barrier to filmmaking in the classroom. For teachers interested in unleashing their students' creativity and concretizing their learning, there has never been a better time to unlock the limitless possibilities video production offers our students.

## Film School

While writing this book, I asked one of my students to film a fun mathematics activity I was teaching. I bravely handed her my phone, not entirely sure what I'd find in my camera roll afterward—a poorly framed shot, the bottom half of my face missing throughout, or perhaps duck-faced selfies with her friends. Instead, I found a well-composed video complete with crash zooms and quick pans for reaction shots. When I asked her where she'd learned such advanced filmmaking techniques, she said, "I think most people just *know* how to shoot video."

I think she's exactly right. For generations, children and adults have sat in front of television screens learning the basic mechanics of shooting video while watching their favorite movies and shows—film school for the masses! However, there's a big difference between capturing video and creating cinema. The process of planning, shooting, and editing a film requires a range of technical competencies in scriptwriting, cinematography, production design, sound mixing, and editing that must be mastered before students can produce narrative or documentary videos worth posting online.

Like audio production, there are three stages of video production: (1) preproduction, (2) production, and (3) postproduction. Each year, I teach my students the essentials of each video production stage through a series of activities I refer to as our very own film school. You are also now entering film school, complete with all the resources I use with my own students. To begin your journey, here are four websites I consistently revisit anytime I need to add to my own filmmaking toolbox.

1. **Film Resources by Grade (https://utahfilmcenter.org/education/film-resources-by-grade):** The Utah Film Center provides media arts education resources and professional development programs for educators looking to integrate film into their instruction. Their resource library of films, short films, and public service announcements is organized by grade level, available to stream for free in the classroom, and includes study guides.

2. **UEN Digital Media Arts (www.uen.org/digitalarts):** The Utah Education Network has curated all the resources needed to navigate the filmmaking process. On their site, they have links to presentations, templates, and videos guiding users through all the steps in preproduction, production, and postproduction, as well as links to other sites with additional teacher tools. My favorite tool to use in class is the Basic Tech for Filmmaking presentation, which includes wonderful examples of pictures, clips, and drawings from films that help students understand some of the more technical filmmaking aspects.

3. **Filmmaking for Everyone (www.learnaboutfilm.com):** Learn About Film is filled with information and advice on the fundamentals of filmmaking: story tips and ideas, equipment lists, understanding film language, and even how to best make films on your phone. It also features unique information not found on most other filmmaking sites, like what photographers need to know about filmmaking. I especially appreciate

the linked videos included in the Poem Films and Film Poems section of the site, which beautifully shows students how music and images can capture and broaden a poem's meaning.

4. **YouTube Creators (www.youtube.com/creators):** YouTube Creators is the official channel supporting content creators who post everything from videos, shorts, livestreams, podcasts, and more on YouTube's platform. They provide best practices and tips from some of the most successful creators online, along with tutorials and how-to videos on everything from lighting design to growing your audience.

In addition to these resources, the digital tools checklist featured in figure 5.1 lists equipment and applications your students will need to complete their video production projects, along with the specific tools my students use in our classroom. The first six digital tools listed are necessities for this section's projects, and the other nine are nice to haves that many students use to elevate the quality of their video productions. You will want to gather this equipment before starting film school.

| Digital Tool Category | Example Tools for This Category |
| --- | --- |
| **Essential Tools** | |
| Computer | Dell Windows laptop and desktop |
| Word processor | Microsoft Word |
| Internet access | School-provided access |
| Microphones | Yeti desktop microphone, PowerDeWise lavalier microphone, RØDE shotgun microphone |
| Cameras | iPhone, Logitech webcam, Canon DSLR |
| Audio editing software | Adobe, Audacity, GarageBand |
| Video editing software | Adobe, Clipchamp, iMovie |
| **Nice-to-Have Tools** | |
| Tripod | Manfrotto |
| Lights | Obeamiu LEDs, ring light |
| Presentation software | PowerPoint, Canva |
| Video conferencing tool | Zoom |
| Computer screen recorder | Loom |
| Teleprompter app | Teleprompter for Video app |
| Green screen | EMART |

**FIGURE 5.1:** Digital tools list.

Visit **go.SolutionTree.com/technology** for a free reproducible version of this figure.

The goal of film school is to equip students with the skills and knowledge needed to create short documentaries, narrative films, and music videos in class. Throughout film school, students complete a series of activities that build their knowledge and skill sets as filmmakers. To graduate, each student must successfully complete a single assignment: the fifteen-second film project. This culminating project challenges students to convey a clear message or story related to a provided theme or prompt in just fifteen seconds. In addition to leveraging all the knowledge and skills they've gained as auteurs, this project requires students to think critically about visual storytelling, effective editing, and efficient communication in a concise format.

Before beginning film school in your classroom, I recommend reviewing the following tips from chapter 1 (page 13) for creating digital content in the classroom just to ensure you have these important pieces in place.

1. Create a digital project folder (page 26).
2. Find your mavens (page 26).
3. Allow speech-to-text (page 29).
4. Translation tools (page 29).
5. Easiest option wins (page 29).

To support your classroom film school, the following sections examine some vital knowledge-building activities to use with your students divided into preproduction, production, and postproduction activities.

## *Preproduction*

Filmmakers will tell you that at least half of the moviemaking process takes place in preproduction. I tell my students to think of filmmaking as a holiday meal: eating the meal is production; cleaning up afterward is postproduction; and the hours spent reading recipes, purchasing food, prepping ingredients, cooking, and burning before the food ever hits the table—that's preproduction. This initial stage is where the film's creative vision takes shape, and student film crews craft their blueprints for these projects, including researching topics, developing scripts, scouting locations, securing the necessary equipment and permissions, and so on. The success of your students' films will depend on how thoroughly and thoughtfully they approach the preproduction process.

### *Activity: Everyone's a Critic*

On the first day of film school, distribute copies of what I call the *Film School Packet*, which is a collection of the following materials found throughout this chapter.

- Fifteen-second film project rubric (figure 5.2, page 82)
- Video production vocabulary sheet (figure 5.3, page 83)
- Everyone's a critic activity (figure 5.4, page 84)
- Fifteen-second film project planning page (figure 5.5, page 85)
- Fifteen-second film project treatment (figure 5.6, page 86)
- Short film screenplay template (figure 5.7, page 89)
- Shot styles cheat sheet (figure 5.8, page 90)
- Shot styles scavenger hunt (figure 5.9, page 92)

- Principles of photography cheat sheet (figure 5.10, page 94)
- One perfect picture guide (figure 5.11, page 95)
- Fifteen-second film project storyboards (figure 5.13, page 96)
- Production roles sheet (figure 5.15, page 99)
- Production cues sheet (figure 5.16, page 99)

Begin this activity by reviewing the fifteen-second film project rubric (figure 5.2) as a class and discussing the characteristics that make a short film successful. In addition, use the video production vocabulary sheet (figure 5.3) to explain any unfamiliar vocabulary words (such as *score*, *a-roll footage*, and *b-roll footage*).

|  | 3 | 2 | 1 |
|---|---|---|---|
| **Content** | The film shares an interesting story or message that moves the audience's thoughts or actions. | The film tells a story or communicates a message to the audience. | The film's story or message is unclear. |
| **Narrative Structure** | The film has an excellent hook that engages the audience with a clear beginning, middle, and end. | The film has a good hook for the audience with some sense of a beginning, middle, and end. | The film lacks an organized structure. |
| **Visuals** | The film is well composed, including a variety of shot styles, lighting, and visual techniques.<br><br>The film makes excellent use of both a-roll and b-roll footage. | The film uses some different shot styles, lighting, and visual techniques.<br><br>The film makes use of both a-roll and b-roll footage. | The film's look is basic and unengaging to the audience.<br><br>The film does not use a-roll and b-roll footage in a thoughtful way. |
| **Audio** | The audio and narrations are high-quality, clear, and easy to understand.<br><br>The score and additional audio enhance the viewing experience and draw the audience into the film. | The audio and narrations can be heard and understood by the audience.<br><br>The score and additional audio are used to enhance the film. | The audio recordings and narrations are low-quality and distracting.<br><br>The score and additional audio detract from the film. |
| **Editing** | Deliberate editing decisions move the film forward from beginning to end.<br><br>The film features seamless integration of transitions, credits, and thoughtful cuts. | Some editing decisions help move the film along.<br><br>The film features transitions, credits, and cuts. | Poor editing leaves the film feeling slow or hard to understand.<br><br>The film features few or no transitions, credits, or cuts. |

**FIGURE 5.2:** *Fifteen-second film project rubric.*

*Visit **go.SolutionTree.com/technology** for a free reproducible version of this figure.*

| Key Vocabulary | Definition |
| --- | --- |
| A-Roll | The primary footage of a film containing the main storyline and actors' performances |
| B-Roll | Secondary footage used to provide context, cutaway shots, or enhance the storytelling and visual appeal of the film |
| Casting | The process of selecting actors for various roles in a film |
| Composition | The arrangement of visual elements within a shot, including framing, angles, and the placement of subjects |
| Continuity | Maintaining consistency with visual elements, such as props, costumes, lighting, and actor positions throughout a film |
| Editing | The process of selecting, arranging, and manipulating filmed footage |
| Green light | The notification that a film project has received approval to move forward into production |
| Logline | A one- or two-sentence summary that succinctly conveys the concept and central conflict of a film |
| Pitch | A presentation in which filmmakers share their ideas for a film |
| Prop | An object that an actor interacts with in a film |
| Reshoot | Refilming specific scenes or shots that did not meet the needs of the film during the initial shoot |
| Rough Cut | An early version of a film's edited footage |
| Safety Shots | Additional shots taken as a precaution to ensure crucial moments are captured correctly and to provide backup options during editing |
| Score | The musical composition that accompanies a film, including background music, themes, and soundtracks |
| Scout | To search for and select suitable filming locations |
| Script | The written narrative of a film, including dialogue, action, and scene descriptions |
| Storyboard | A series of illustrated panels that visually represent important shots or scenes in a film, serving as a filmmaker's visual plan |
| Treatment | A written summary of a film's characters, plot, themes, and visual elements |

**FIGURE 5.3:** *Video production vocabulary sheet.*

*Visit **go.SolutionTree.com/technology** for a free reproducible version of this figure.*

Next, students watch three fifteen-second films from the models provided in the following list.

- **And what are you supposed to be? (www.youtube.com/watch?v=_nGAP6G2xr8):** When a woman answers the door on Halloween, she finds ghosts on her doorstep. My students love scary movies, and this one doesn't disappoint!
- **McDonald's commercial (www.youtube.com/watch?v=oqpfgUQET6A):** A woman sits down to eat with a man she thought was her boyfriend. This is a great example of how filmmakers can use stories to sell a particular idea and product.
- **Jumper action scene (www.youtube.com/watch?v=e5hY6WMDXrw):** A young man must use his special powers to disarm the man chasing him. The special effects in this short are super cool, and yet it feels like students made it.
- **Fifteen-second film festival compilation (www.15SecondFilmFestival.com):** This compilation of fifteen-second films has some gems, including a racecar driving grandma and a child drawing a masterpiece in the condensation on his window.

Afterward, students should complete the everyone's a critic activity by rating each film out of fifteen and writing a short review as if they were film critics (figure 5.4). At the end of the lesson, preview the fifteen-second film project planning page (figure 5.5) so students have a clear sense of where film school is taking them.

---

**Directions:** Imagine you are a film critic assigned to review a new collection of fifteen-second films. After watching each video, use the fifteen-second film project rubric to give the film a score out of fifteen and write a short review, including what you appreciated most about each film or what you would have done differently if you were the director.

Film 1: _____  Score: _____ /15

Review:

_____

_____

_____

Film 2: _____  Score: _____ /15

Review:

_____

_____

_____

Film 3: _____  Score: _____ /15

Review:

_____

_____

_____

---

**FIGURE 5.4:** *Everyone's a critic activity.*

*Visit **go.SolutionTree.com/technology** for a free reproducible version of this figure.*

| **Filmmaker:** | **Fifteen-Second Film Title:** |
|---|---|
| **Preproduction** ||
| Step 1: Complete a treatment for the script. ||
| Step 2: Draft the script. ||
| Step 3: Create storyboards for the film. ||
| **Production** ||
| Step 4: Shoot primary (a-roll) and secondary (b-roll) footage. ||
| Step 5: Record additional audio, including narration or sound effects. ||
| **Postproduction** ||
| Step 6: Edit the film: video, still images, narration, music, transitions, effects, and credits. ||
| Step 7: Screen the rough cut for at least two critical friends, who will each give you a score with the rubric and a Critical Friend Feedback Form. Continue editing as needed. ||
| Step 8: Present the final product during the fifteen-second film festival. ||
| Step 9: Complete an After-Project Reflection. ||

**FIGURE 5.5:** *Fifteen-second film project planning page.*

*Visit **go.SolutionTree.com/technology** for a free reproducible version of this figure.*

### Activity: Fifteen-Second Film Project Treatment

The next phase of film school is all about screenwriting and helping students get their stories on paper. Have students open their packets to the fifteen-second film project treatment (figure 5.6, page 86) and outline the essential elements of their own short films.

Most of my students' film concepts are drawn directly from journal entries and short stories they have written throughout the year. However, if your students need help brainstorming ideas, here are some questions you can ask to help stir their imaginations.

- Do you have a personal story that you think would make a great short film?
- What emotions or moods do you want your audience to feel while watching your film?
- Do you have a favorite film genre you'd like to explore?
- Picture a main character for your story. What motivates them? What are they trying to accomplish?
- Is there a unique location or time that you find interesting or that inspires you?
- What's one obstacle that your character(s) might need to overcome?
- Can you think of an opening shot that would immediately hook an audience?

### Activity: Write Your Script

Writing a screenplay is a unique and creative way to tell a story. A *screenplay* is defined as a story told with pictures painted in dialogue and descriptions within the context of dramatic structure (Field, 1984). For students to write a screenplay—even a really short one—they'll need an understanding of the specific format, structure, and elements that make up a successful screenplay.

| Directions: It's time to transition from critic to creator. Now that you have watched and reviewed several videos, write an outline for your own film on this fifteen-second film project treatment. ||
|---|---|
| Characters: | Setting: |

| Introduction and conflict: |
|---|

| Plot events: |
|---|

| Climax: |
|---|

| Resolution: |
|---|

| Genre: | Theme: | Logline: |
|---|---|---|

**FIGURE 5.6:** Fifteen-second film project treatment.

Visit **go.SolutionTree.com/technology** *for a free reproducible version of this figure.*

First, though, I want to be clear that your students can write their scripts using whatever format *you* are most comfortable with. For example, maybe you just want them to type their scripts in a word processor document as they would for a short story such as the following.

*At the end of a long day at school, the kids at Meadowlark Elementary ran out the doors of the school. Tal, Ismail, and Kyaw trailed behind.*

*"What did y'all get on the test, then?" Ismail asked.*

*"Uhhh, 94 percent," Kyaw said, not entirely sure.*

*"Darn, I got 80 percent!" Tal laughed.*

You can also have students follow the reader's theater format they've likely seen in their English language arts textbooks since they were younger:

*At the end of a long day at school, the kids at Meadowlark Elementary ran out the doors of the school. Tal, Ismail, and Kyaw trailed behind.*

**ISMAIL:** *What did y'all get on the test, then?*

**KYAW (unsure):** *Uhhh, 94 percent.*

**TAL (laughing):** *Darn, I got 80 percent!*

Still, it's so fun writing a screenplay like the pros. The standard screenplay format isn't hard to learn, but it does involve a specific set of rules and guidelines that screenwriters follow to ensure consistency and clarity in presenting the story to the reader, director, and actors. The following list highlights the key elements.

- Page layout:
    - Paper size: Use standard letter-size paper (8.5" × 11") with one-inch margins on all sides.
    - Font: Use Courier or Courier New, 12-point font size.
    - Double-spacing: Double-space the entire screenplay, including dialogue, action, and scene headings.
    - Page numbers: Number each page consecutively in the top-right corner.
- Scene headings:
    - Location: Use scene headings to indicate the location—interior versus exterior, as well as where the scene is taking place—and the time of day.
    - Style: Capitalize and start on the left margin of the page, as in the following example.
      ```
      INT. COFFEE SHOP—DAY
      ```
- Descriptions:
    - Paragraphs are concise and use present tense.
    - Active and descriptive language paints a vivid picture in the reader's mind.
    - Action paragraphs describe what is happening in the scene, including physical movements, reactions, and the environment.
    - Character names are capitalized the first time they are introduced, as in the following example.
      ```
      JOHN sits nervously at the table, tapping his fingers.
      His eyes dart around the room, searching for someone.
      ```

- Dialogue:
    - Present dialogue as a text block centered on the page with the character's name in uppercase.
    - Use parentheses, known as parentheticals, to provide emotional context for the dialogue and instructions for how the lines should be delivered, as in the following.

    ```
                    JOHN (whispering)
          I can't believe you didn't tell me.
                         SARA
       If I had told you, we wouldn't be having this
                  conversation right now.
    ```
- Transitions:
    - Transitions signal the passage of time or a change in location between scenes.
    - Transitions act as notes to the film's editor and help the reader understand how the story will flow visually on the screen.
    - Common transitions include CUT TO:, FADE IN:, FADE OUT:, DISSOLVE TO:, and so on. See the following example.

    ```
    FADE IN: INT. COFFEE SHOP—DAY
    ```

To begin this activity, have students turn to the short film screenplay template (figure 5.7). Because I teach upper elementary–age students, I also pass out a model script from the first minute of the Pixar movie *Toy Story* as my model. You can search for sample script excerpts online or reproduce your own version of a short scene for students.

Read the script together and discuss how your students might shoot this scene if they were directing the live-action remake of the film (camera angles, zooming in and out on characters, and delivery of dialogue, for example). Then, watch the scene from the actual film and compare the words on the page with the visuals that made it to the screen. On the other side of the page, students draft their own script using the professional screenplay format. Following the outline in their treatment, students must introduce the setting, characters, and action in their film's opening and then continue with the remaining script.

The last step in this activity is having students type their screenplay drafts on the computer. Some teachers use dedicated screenwriting software like Final Draft that automatically formats manuscripts for students; I personally just have my students type their drafts as word processor documents. The only thing that's tricky in a word processor is getting the dialogue to center on the page in a narrow column, which I mostly avoid by telling my writers to center and boldface their dialogue and let it stretch across the page. Still, I always have at least one student who will hit enter, backspace, and tab as many times as they must to make their screenplay look like it was drafted by Francis Ford Coppola. Formatting is useful for achieving uniformity across projects, which makes life easier for both teacher and student; however, as long as the text clearly communicates the student's vision, I wouldn't get hung up on screenwriting rules.

### *Activity: Shot Styles Scavenger Hunt*

When writing prose, students use a variety of sentence types to avoid monotony and convey different tones and moods to their readers. As filmmakers, students must use different shot styles

**Write Your Script**

INT. or EXT.   _____   — DAY or NIGHT
(Circle One)                                (LOCATION)                                   (Circle One)

Introduce the setting, characters, and action: What will the audience see on screen? What does this place look like? Describe your characters. What are they doing?

_____

_____

_____

_____

_____

_____

Now, write your screenplay! When a character talks, write it like this:

CHARACTER NAME
_____

Draft Screenplay (continue on additional sheets of paper):

_____

_____

_____

_____

_____

_____

_____

_____

**FIGURE 5.7:** *Short film screenplay template.*

*Visit **go.SolutionTree.com/technology** for a free reproducible version of this figure.*

for these same reasons. Different shot styles add visual variety to films and can be used to communicate information to the audience by emphasizing emotions, foreshadowing events, building tension, and revealing characters' inner thoughts.

In this activity, students first learn twelve of the most common shot styles used in photography and films, listed here on the shot styles cheat sheet shown in figure 5.8 (page 90).

Different shot styles add visual variety to films. They can emphasize emotions, draw our attention, foreshadow events, build tension, and reveal characters' inner thoughts.

Wide Shot (Establishing Shot)

Over-the-Shoulder Shot

Long Shot (Master Shot)

High-Angle Shot

Medium Shot

Low-Angle Shot

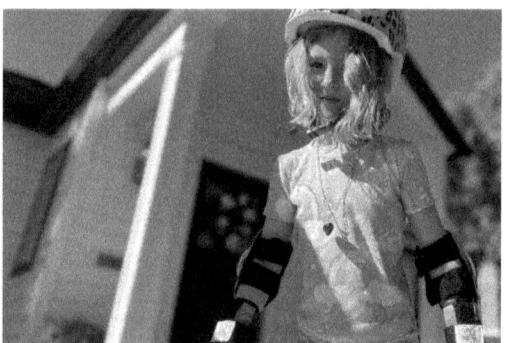

Two Shot

Dutch Angle Shot

**FIGURE 5.8:** *Shot styles cheat sheet.*

*Visit **go.SolutionTree.com/technology** for a free reproducible version of this figure.*

Any of the following resources can be used for teaching shot styles to prepare students for this activity. I typically use the first video because it includes beautifully composed examples of each shot style on the list.

- Full-Time Filmmaker: 12 Camera Angles to Enhance Your Films (www.youtube.com/watch?v=SlNviMsi0K0)
- Studio Binder: The Ultimate Guide to Camera Shots (www.studiobinder.com/blog/ultimate-guide-to-camera-shots)
- Types of Shots: Tomorrow's Filmmakers (www.youtube.com/watch?v=wU3gJd8BGBo)
- Different Types of Shots in Film (https://tinyurl.com/33mtkanr)

Then, students take their own photos, gathering at least one example of each type in the shot styles scavenger hunt shown in figure 5.9 (page 92). I have my students use their laptop cameras to take the pictures and then paste the images on a blank scavenger hunt page, usually in a document, digital notebook (like Microsoft OneNote or Google Keep) or even a presentation slide—any digital workspace where students can organize and sort their photographs will do the job.

**Directions:** Using your laptop camera or mobile device, gather at least one example of each shot style. Insert your photos into the correct boxes on this page.

| Wide Shot (Establishing Shot) | Over-the-Shoulder Shot |
|---|---|
| Long Shot (Master Shot) | High-Angle Shot |
| Medium Shot | Low-Angle Shot |
| Two Shot | Dutch Angle Shot |

| Close-Up Shot | Point-of-View Shot |
|---|---|
| Extreme Close-Up Shot | Cutaway Shot |

**FIGURE 5.9:** *Shot styles scavenger hunt.*

*Visit **go.SolutionTree.com/technology** for a free reproducible version of this figure.*

### Activity: One Perfect Pic

In addition to using various shot styles and angles, cinematographers rely on other composition principles to create lovely shots. You could deeply immerse yourself in studying all existing principles, but for the purposes of film school and the kinds of video production your students will engage in, I recommend focusing on just three: (1) depth of field, (2) key light, and (3) the rule of thirds. Each of these is defined for students in the cheat sheet in figure 5.10 (page 94).

For this activity, students have a seemingly simple task: take one perfect picture by following the directions shown in figure 5.11 (page 95). This picture should demonstrate their ability to use depth of field, a key light, and the rule of thirds in their visual composition. The depth of field can be shallow or deep, the key light can be a window or the sun, and the rule of thirds can be adhered to or broken—what matters is that cinematographers *intentionally* make these choices, and so must our students.

### Activity: Storyboards

With their screenplay complete, each filmmaker must storyboard their film. A storyboard, as depicted in figure 5.12 (page 95), is a graphic organizer that incorporates illustrations and text in a series of panels to help filmmakers previsualize the shots they need to capture during filming.

With so little time in the day, this would be an easy step for teachers and students to skip; however, storyboarding brings a high return on investment for students. It clarifies a film crew's

| Cinematography Principles | Example |
|---|---|
| Depth of field refers to the range of distances within a frame that are in sharp focus. A shallow depth of field means that only a small portion of a frame is in focus, isolating a subject from the background and emphasizing its importance. A deep depth of field keeps a larger area in focus, keeping more of the entire image sharp and clear. | |
| The key light is the primary light source in a frame and should be strategically positioned to illuminate the subject, defining its shape and form. By manipulating the key light's intensity, direction, and quality, the key light can control shadows and create dimension, contrast, and mood in a shot. | |
| The rule of thirds divides an image into nine equal parts using two horizontal and two vertical lines, creating a grid. Important elements are placed off-center along these lines or at their intersections rather than at the center of the frame to make a shot more dynamic, inviting viewers to explore the entire frame. | |

**FIGURE 5.10**: *Principles of photography cheat sheet.*

Visit **go.SolutionTree.com/technology** *for a free reproducible version of this figure.*

collective vision for a film, centers conversations during preproduction and production, helps identify potential problems or limitations in the script, and optimizes production schedules, leading to a smoother, more efficient filmmaking experience.

To keep it simple, I tell my students to storyboard only the most memorable moments of their films on their fifteen-second film project storyboards (see figure 5.13, page 96)—the shots that must be just right for their story to work. The drawings don't need to be perfect, just clear in their vision—I prefer when my students draw stick figures. Student storyboards are meant to save time, so don't allow your students to waste time trying to make them *amazing*.

Digital Videos 101     95

**Directions:** Staple a picture to this page demonstrating your ability to use depth of field, key light, and the rule of thirds. Answer the following questions about your composition.

1. Is the depth of field in your picture deep or shallow? Explain how you know and why you chose this creative composition.

2. What source of illumination did you use for your key light? Why did you use this light source, and how does it create dimension, contrast, or mood in this shot?

3. How does your picture adhere to or break the rule of thirds? How did you decide where to position your subject within the frame?

**FIGURE 5.11**: One perfect picture guide.

Visit **go.SolutionTree.com/technology** for a free reproducible version of this figure.

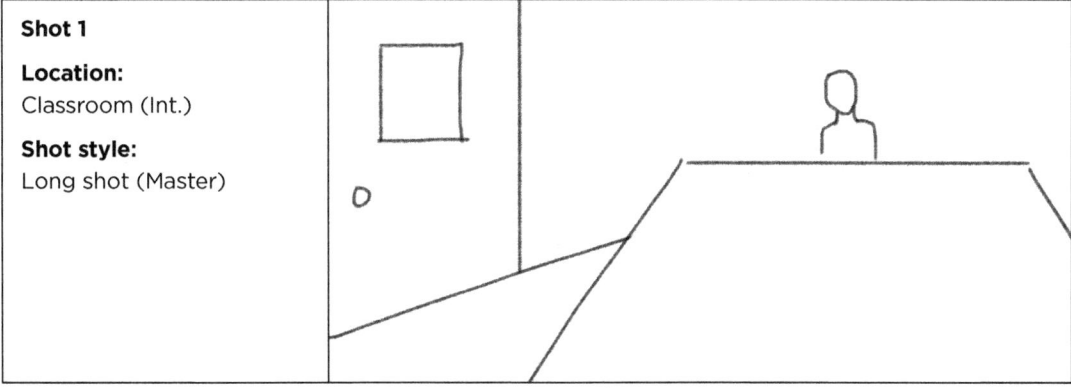

**FIGURE 5.12**: Storyboard example.

Visit **go.SolutionTree.com/technology** for a free reproducible version of this figure.

**Directions:** Illustrate four simple storyboards for the most memorable moments in your fifteen-second film project. Draw from the angle of the shot style you plan to use and include any characters or props that will be part of the shot.

| | |
|---|---|
| **Shot 1**<br>**Location:**<br><br>**Shot Style:** | |
| **Shot 2**<br>**Location:**<br><br>**Shot Style:** | |
| **Shot 3**<br>**Location:**<br><br>**Shot Style:** | |
| **Shot 4**<br>**Location:**<br><br>**Shot Style:** | |

**FIGURE 5.13**: *Fifteen-second film project storyboards.*

*Visit **go.SolutionTree.com/technology** for a free reproducible version of this figure.*

During preproduction, students should also begin scouting locations where they will be shooting their fifteen-second films. Taking time to scout locations during preproduction allows filmmakers to arrive on set with less stress and specific framed shots in mind, so everyone is ready to film efficiently with the available time. Students filming in school must secure permission to shoot in their scouted locations, including specific times and dates. Prior to filming, they also need to confirm the location is still available and profusely thank whoever is allowing them to film there. For off-site locations, filmmakers must also secure the proper permissions and, depending on their age, should share with you the contact information of the parents, caretakers, or other adults who will be supervising and supporting them during their shoot.

## Production

Congratulations! You and your students have made it through preproduction, which means you are now in the production stage of film school. Your young filmmakers are finally ready to begin shooting their fifteen-second films. Now they'll need access to whatever film equipment you have available. The only two must-have pieces of equipment each student will need are a camera and a microphone, which are now included on all smartphones, tablets, and laptop computers. Again, the other equipment—lights, props, tripods, fancier cameras, and mics—are all nice to haves and can often be checked out through your school's multimedia center, your district's educational technology department, or local nonprofits and film centers. While this equipment may improve the overall quality of your students' films, brilliant films are often made better by sticking with the simplest tools.

These fifteen-second films aren't meant to be masterpieces—they are designed to demonstrate technical competency, not win an Oscar. At the same time, it's a beautiful thing when students care enough about a project to make it the best it can be. So, if your students are going to check out equipment, shoot in locations in and out of school, and capture more footage than they could ever possibly need for a fifteen-second film, here are five tips to keep things cool, calm, and collected throughout your film-school production.

1. Maintain an updated sign-out sheet (see figure 5.14, page 98) and only check out equipment to your most reliable and trustworthy students.

2. As video is shot and captured on phones or memory cards, provide each student with a digital project folder (see "Digital Tools and Technology Tips;" chapter 1, page 25) on their computer for storing their footage and any other images, audio, and so on, needed for their film. Make sure students clearly understand where their project folders are located, how they are labeled, and how to transfer media files in and out of them.

3. Students can only shoot at locations they have scouted ahead of time. Arriving on location with shots already planned within that space saves time and improves the production experience for everyone.

4. If students are filming during school, only one student filmmaker and their cast can shoot outside of the classroom at a time. I post a simple shooting calendar where students can sign up for specific dates, times, and locations in the school.

5. Encourage students to shoot at least one safety shot (additional take) for each critical shot. This helps ensure that when they edit their footage, they have everything they need and won't require a reshoot.

| Equipment Information | Borrower Information || Borrowed || Returned ||
|---|---|---|---|---|---|---|
| | Name | Team | Date | Initial | Date | Initial |
| | | | | | | |
| | | | | | | |
| | | | | | | |
| | | | | | | |

**FIGURE 5.14**: *Digital equipment sign-out sheet.*
Visit **go.SolutionTree.com/technology** *for a free reproducible version of this figure.*

Filmmaking is a wonderfully collaborative art form, and your students will need to fill a variety of production roles on future projects. However, for these fifteen-second films, they are a crew of one—director, cinematographer, and editor. Still, one of the best parts about making films in class is listening to students picturing themselves working in the movie industry one day. That's why, just before they start shooting, I introduce them to the production roles sheet shown in figure 5.15, which lists some of the most common jobs on a Hollywood movie set. I also love showing them the production cues sheet in figure 5.16 and all the commands they might get to shout at work someday. Both sheets highlight in bold the roles and cues students will need for their film projects after film school. To increase efficiency and add some fun on set, make sure each student film crew has a director, cinematographer, sound designer, and grip, and that they're regularly throwing out industry terms like, *quiet on set, rolling,* and *action*!

| Production Roles | Definition |
|---|---|
| **Cinematographer** | Oversees photography and camera work on a film, including lighting and framing, to achieve the film's desired look. |
| Composer | Creates the musical score or selects existing music for the film. |
| Costume designer | Creates or selects costumes that fit the characters and the film's time period or setting. |
| **Director** | Brings the script to life on screen. Oversees all departments and works with actors on their performances. |
| **Assistant editor** | Oversees day-to-day tasks of the cutting room. |
| **Editor** | Assembles the footage to create a coherent and engaging film. |
| **Gaffer** | Oversees lighting and all things that require power. |

| | |
|---|---|
| **Grip** | Oversees all equipment on set that doesn't require power. |
| Producer | Oversees all aspects of a film project, from development to distribution. |
| Production designer | Oversees the film's visual elements, including sets, props, costumes, and the overall production design. |
| Screenwriter | Writes or adapts scripts for films. |
| **Sound designer** | Works on the auditory elements of a film, including sound effects, foley, and the overall soundscape. |
| Stunt coordinator | Plans and executes action sequences and stunts safely. |

**FIGURE 5.15**: Production roles sheet.

Visit **go.SolutionTree.com/technology** for a free reproducible version of this figure.

| **Production Cues** | **Translation** |
|---|---|
| **Action** | Begin. |
| Background | People in the background, start moving. |
| Check the gate | Make sure there's nothing on the camera lens. |
| **Cut** | Stop. |
| Cutting room floor | That footage won't make it into the movie. |
| Martini shot | This is the last shot of the day. |
| Moving on | Let's move on to the next scene. |
| One more time | Do it again. |
| **Quiet on set** | Everybody, be quiet. |
| Reset | Put everything back how it was. |
| **Rolling** | Camera and sound are recording. |
| Standby | Wait. |
| **Wrap** | We're done. |

**FIGURE 5.16**: Production cues sheet.

Visit **go.SolutionTree.com/technology** for a free reproducible version of this figure.

### Activity: Shoot Video and Record Audio

They have their scripts. They have their storyboards. Your students know where they're shooting, what they're shooting, and how to get it done. At this point, your job is to facilitate and troubleshoot as your filmmakers independently shoot their fifteen-second films. Remind students to use the cinematography principles they've learned to compose their shots and support them when they inevitably stumble.

Most students will capture their footage quickly, and only a handful will record additional audio beyond what is captured by the device they're filming on. That's *good*! This isn't the project; this is how students prove they're ready to *move on* to the project. In other words, this isn't the road trip; it's the road test.

That said, you and your students still want these films to be good, and nothing ruins a film faster than bad audio. Here are four tips for helping students record awesome audio.

1. Eliminate as much background noise as possible before filming.
2. Record thirty seconds of ambient sound to lay over any gaps or b-roll footage in postproduction.
3. Use external mics whenever possible.
4. Record voiceover narration in a small, silent room to avoid echoes and ambient sounds.

Once students have uploaded all their footage and audio into their digital project folder, it's time for them to enter the final stage of film school: postproduction.

## Postproduction

There's an old saying in filmmaking: *first, you shoot the movie, and then you make the movie*. Your students have planned, executed, and gathered all their visual and auditory ingredients together. Now, it's time to combine those pieces into a well-told story.

In chapter 4 (page 61), students learned how to use audio editing software to cut, trim, and edit clips; remove unwanted noises, mistakes, or pauses; and then reassemble what remained into a polished audio production. Now, your students will use those same skills in the video editing platform you have available for them. If you're not sure what video editing software your school or district has loaded on its devices, reach out to your school's media specialist or IT person, and they should be able to help you. If your school or district does not provide a video editing software interface, there are free online video editing platforms, including Vimeo, Canva, Adobe Express, YouTube, and WeVideo. Whatever platform you choose, they are all designed to be relatively intuitive, and instructional videos are available online to help you learn how to use their tools. Furthermore, all video editing software programs use common program elements like the following.

- **Library or clip bin:** This is a space where media is initially imported into the editing software.
- **Timeline:** This is the central workspace where filmmakers arrange, edit, and sequence video clips, audio tracks, and other media.
- **Player or preview window:** This is where the current frame or video segment being edited is displayed.
- **Task pane:** This is the window that contains tools to import media; add text, titles, credits, and transitions; and export the final film as a video file.
- **Audio controls:** This is where editors can adjust audio levels, add music or sound effects, and manipulate audio tracks.

The following sections offer three activities to support your students' postproduction efforts.

### Activity: Edit the Fifteen-Second Film

Editing a film is like putting together a one-thousand-piece puzzle—some people like working on the whole thing at once, and others prefer focusing on one small section at a time. Similarly, there are two strategies I teach my students for constructing their films once everyone imports their files into the video editing software.

- **Option 1:** Drag *all* the media files onto the timeline and move the pieces around until the full story reveals itself.
- **Option 2:** Thoughtfully drag each media file onto the timeline one at a time and fit the pieces together as you go.

Both options have proven successful in my classroom; it just depends on how each editor prefers to process and synthesize information. Thankfully, after plotting out their stories in pre-production and fleshing out their films during production, students usually enter this stage with a clear understanding of how these pieces should all fit together.

The true work of an editor is less in telling the story than it is in *crafting* the story. They painstakingly examine the impact that adding a fraction of a second of video might have on the film's overall flow. Editing can be tedious, meticulous work, and that's why some creators *love* it. From the first day of school, I'm always on the lookout for students who can't stand to color outside the lines, who use a ruler to rip a piece of paper, or who lean in really close when cutting with scissors—those students are my editors.

There's no better way to learn the ins and outs of editing than by simply doing it, and most students show up these days having already spliced together countless video clips and pictures on social media platforms. Let your students play with the platform, encourage them to take risks, answer whatever questions you can, and enjoy finding answers together for the ones you can't.

Students usually don't think about their film's audio and music until after they've finished editing their video clips in the timeline; once that's done, ask them these three questions.

1. Is there any additional audio you need to capture (sound effects, voiceover narration, and so on)?
2. Do you want to rerecord any sections of bad dialogue (dialogue that is too quiet, too loud, can't be understood, and so on)?
3. Do you want to add music to your film?

Not every student wants music in their film, but I encourage all of them to at least import one track while in film school just for practice. Most students naturally understand when a piece of music is tonally or thematically a nice match for their film, but I love facilitating conversations about music by scoring my young filmmakers' works with my own horrible musical selections (think carnival music or a funeral dirge). By playfully discussing the kinds of music that don't serve their film, students can more easily articulate the musical elements that would connect with audiences and elevate their films.

If students wish to use copyrighted music in their short videos, they most likely can do so because of fair use, which allows limited use for educational purposes in educational settings (see pages 20–22 for more information). However, if you want to be sure you are steering clear of any potential copyright violations, here are some useful open-source and royalty-free music sites students can use to locate music for their productions.

- **The Free Music Archive (https://freemusicarchive.org):** This site offers free access to open-licensed, original music by independent artists around the world to play, download, and share.

- **Musopen (https://musopen.org):** This site seeks to "set music free" by providing an online library of public domain music recordings, sheet music, and textbooks to the public for free, without copyright restrictions.
- **The YouTube Audio Library (www.studio.youtube.com):** This site provides royalty-free production, copyright-safe music, and sound effects to download and use in your videos.

### Activity: Screen Your Rough Cut

Nothing slows work down in the editing room more than students wanting their friends to see some small change they've made to their film. The shout of, "Hey, come check this out!" is super adorable and can also spark some great ideas among peers that improve each other's films; however, I encourage my students to hold off on sharing their work with one another until they have a rough cut ready to screen.

A *rough cut* is the first draft of a film, and, as with any written piece, students need positive and productive feedback on their first draft to move toward a much-improved final draft. I keep it simple for this activity. I tell my students, "Once your rough cut is ready, pick two friends to show it to and discuss your fifteen-second film using the fifteen-second film project rubric and the 'Critical Friend Feedback Form' to guide your conversation" (figure 5.2, page 82, and page 157 in the appendix, respectively). This way, the filmmaker receives valuable feedback, and their friends return to their work with new ideas for their own films.

### Activity: The Fifteen-Second Film Festival

During an interview, George Lucas said, "Films are never finished; they're only abandoned" (Quoteresearch, 2019). If I let them, most of my students would continuously revise their short films until they ran out of days in the school year. However, there are bigger and better projects to tackle, messages that must be shared, and stories that need to be told. So, after only a couple of days in the editing room, it's time to premiere their films at their very own fifteen-second film festival.

Yes, calling this a film festival is overselling it. While it's more of a gallery stroll where students wander around the room watching each other's films, don't hesitate to look for ways to liven up the experience for your students. If I'm feeling sparky, I bring juice and cookies. After all the hard work you and your students have put into completing film school, what's most important is the public exhibition and celebration of their creative achievements. It is deserved and always a hit.

Before your digital content creators move onto the bigger projects outlined in part II—producing documentaries, short films, or music videos—it's important for them to reflect on the technical and creative lessons they've learned in film school. By completing an "After-Project Reflection Form" (page 157 in the appendix), students examine what they appreciated in their own work, what might have been improved had they made different choices, and what they will do moving forward to take their creative process and films to the next level.

## Amplifying Student Voices: Online Video-Sharing Platforms

Will your students beg you to post their fifteen-second film projects online for the world to see? Maybe, but probably not. However, with the skills your students develop during film school, they will create documentaries, narrative films, music videos, and other digital content that audiences will want to see.

First, as discussed throughout this book, make sure you're consistently communicating with parents and administrators so they are fully aware of the incredible projects coming together in your class. Also, it's critical that every student has a signed media release form (see figure I.3, page 9, in the introduction) turned in, because once you post their videos online, you are responsible for safeguarding their work and identities in an often-perilous landscape. This can be daunting enough with blog posts and podcasts, but with their faces appearing online, it's more important than ever that you secure permission and take every precaution. But don't forget— this is all worth it for the opportunity to amplify their brilliance and empower their young voices.

If you are especially concerned for student safety and privacy, here is a list of online video-sharing platforms that account for factors like data security, privacy controls, and content moderation.

1. **School-approved learning management systems:** Platforms like Canvas and Moodle offer secure environments for sharing and managing student videos. These systems are typically integrated with the school's IT infrastructure and prioritize student privacy.
2. **Private YouTube channels:** Create a private YouTube channel restricted to a specific group of students, parents, and educators. Only those with the link can access the content. YouTube provides some privacy controls, but it's essential to educate students on responsible use.
3. **Vimeo privacy settings:** Vimeo provides more robust privacy features than YouTube, allowing users to set privacy controls and limit video access to specific users or utilize password protection.

YouTube and Vimeo are probably the two best-known online video-sharing platforms, and they both have solid pros in their favor. For YouTube, consider the following.

1. **Large audience:** With billions of global users, YouTube has a massive potential audience for students.
2. **Searchability:** Thanks to YouTube's search algorithm, it's easy for viewers to discover and share students' work, leading to greater exposure for their stories and messages.
3. **Free hosting:** YouTube provides free hosting for videos, making it a no-cost option for teachers and students.
4. **Community engagement:** YouTube allows for comments and interaction with viewers, building a community around student content. However, those comments can also be turned off and interactions eliminated for students' safety.

The one big drawback of YouTube is that it features ads that can contain inappropriate content depending on your students' age.

As for Vimeo, the following features highlight its pros.

1. **Privacy controls:** As mentioned, Vimeo's privacy settings allow you to choose who can access your videos, including password protection, domain-level privacy, and more.
2. **No ads:** Vimeo doesn't include ads in videos, providing a distraction-free viewing experience, which is more suited for student-generated content.
3. **High-quality playback:** Vimeo prioritizes video quality, which is why many professional videographers prefer it over YouTube.
4. **Customer support:** Having the ability to reach out to customer support is a gift for students and teachers in need of technical assistance.

Vimeo's one big drawback is it has a much smaller user base than YouTube, making it harder to gain a broader audience or recognition.

## Conclusion

My students publish their films on our class's YouTube channel, @9thEvermore. I tell them from the start of the school year that we are creating films to be shared and viewed publicly because the information and stories they contain are important and need to be known. However, my filmmakers and crews decide together whether they want their films posted publicly on YouTube or privately so only those they trust with the link can view their films. Interestingly, almost all film crews have chosen to post their team projects privately over the years; I think it's because their films, especially the documentaries, are deeply personal projects, and they want some say in who gets to watch them. All students deserve that level of control over the viewership and dissemination of their creative works—self-determination is the defining characteristic of an empowered student voice. At the same time, film is a collaborative art form, and students respect that they each have the artistic right to share their collective work with whoever they choose.

Either way, we teachers must take our cues on how loudly we should amplify our students' content from how tightly they hold onto it. Obviously, if students want to keep their work private, then we must honor that decision, no matter how brilliant that work may be. If, however, students want to share what they've made with the world, then we need to shout their stories from the virtual rooftops and send that content far and wide.

It reminds me of my favorite thing to say when a student asks me, "What are we going to do today?"

"Hard to say, who knows how things will go? But how about this—you lead, I'll follow."

# CHAPTER 6

# Documentary Short Films

**PROJECT OBJECTIVE**

I will empower my students' voices by teaching them to share information, raise awareness, and advocate for positive change through film.

**Definition of Documentary**

**noun**
(Of a movie, a television or radio program, or photography) using pictures or interviews with people involved in real events to provide a factual record or report.

**adjective**
Consisting of official pieces of written, printed, or other matter.

*—Oxford English Dictionary Online*

## CREATORS AT WORK

"Are you *sure* you want to make a documentary about growing up without a dad in your life?"

"Yep, we're sure. And we already know our title—*Daughters Without Fathers*."

Anna and Tina hated each other in fifth grade because Tina wore makeup and Anna didn't. The next year, they were best friends. I don't know when they realized they'd both lost their dads to crime and deportation, but when it came time to make short documentary films in class, they knew the story they wanted to tell.

"This film will let other girls in our same situation know that they aren't alone," Tina said. "I'm OK with talking about messed up things that happened in my life, and so is Anna. We just want to help. Maybe we can't stop fathers from leaving their families, but at least we can let people know this is a serious problem!"

My palms began sweating as I listened to the girls describe the film they wanted to make. When they finished pitching their concept, I let them know what I thought.

"Honestly, this film concept makes me nervous. You'll have to dig deep in your interviews and conversations and spend *a lot* of time intensely focused on emotionally and psychologically difficult things. I think it's beautiful that you want to make this film to help other girls like you, but are you sure you don't just want to make a film about your love for BTS or the history of the steering wheel instead?"

The girls laughed and looked at one another, nodding in agreement. Still unsure, I read through their film treatment one more time.

"All right, your project is greenlit. However, I want you to find another student to join your team. You need someone to help conduct your interviews, run the camera, and check sound, among other things, so you can both focus on telling your story."

A serious look came over Anna's face. "Eve could join us, but her dad's still here and lives with her. Is that all right?"

I couldn't help but smile. "Of course! Kids who aren't in your situation are going to benefit from watching your film, too, and Eve will get the added benefit of sharing this journey with you. Also, keep this in mind." I pointed at the table with the documentary rubric shown in figure 6.1.

"Look where it says, 'Research and Interviews.' As you share details from your personal life in this film, you'll also be providing qualitative evidence through your interviews in support of your claim that there are a lot of girls out there, especially the daughters of immigrants, who are enduring the same hardships you are. You're raising awareness for an issue—daughters without fathers—that should matter to *all* of us, not just the girls directly affected. This film makes me nervous because it's important, its purpose is clear, and it will require so much from you. Do you understand?"

Tina and Anna both sat up in their chairs. I remember thinking their seats suddenly looked a little small for them, like they weren't made to fit the young ladies sitting in them now.

Scan the QR code and watch these young women share their personal stories so girls like them can know they're not alone.

**THESE DAYS, WHEN A** baby is born, its documentary film begins. As a society, we're all obsessed with documenting our lives. Whether it's taking pictures of a pretty meal, recording a video of our children being hilarious, or editing together a montage for an Instagram reel, we can't stop capturing the moments that make up the story of our lives. My phone's camera roll looks like the endless warehouse in *Indiana Jones and the Raiders of the Lost Ark*—its dusty shelves are filled with countless pictures and videos I'm too lazy to delete but will happily scroll through when I ought to be going to bed.

Documentary films tell nonfiction stories about events, social or cultural issues, communities, places, or people. Like narrative films, the story in a documentary typically follows a narrative arc or three-act structure (beginning, middle, and end). They use effective visual storytelling techniques, including video with a variety of shot styles, still images (photographs, stock images, magazine or newspaper clippings, and personal artwork), interviews, voiceover narration, music, sound effects, animations, and text (Mallory, Montgomery, Ringo, & Wray, 2018).

Documentarians are dedicated to asking and answering their own questions, researching their topics, studying their subjects, building their cases, and interviewing anyone with expertise, experience, or power. They disseminate information, tell great stories, and persuade others to make

|  | 3 | 2 | 1 |
| --- | --- | --- | --- |
| **Storytelling and Structure** | The film shares an interesting story or message that moves the audience's thoughts or actions.<br><br>The film has an excellent hook that engages the audience with a clear beginning, middle, and end. | The film tells a story or communicates a message to the audience.<br><br>The film has a good hook for the audience and some sense of a beginning, middle, and end. | The film's story or message is unclear.<br><br>The film lacks an organized structure. |
| **Research and Interviews** | Quantitative and qualitative information thoughtfully support the film's story or message.<br><br>High-quality interview questions draw compelling answers that add to the film's story or message. | Quantitative and qualitative information is present in the film.<br><br>Good questions are answered by the interview subjects. | Little to no quantitative or qualitative information is used in the film.<br><br>Interviews add little to the film's story or message. |
| **Visuals** | A variety of shot styles, lighting, and visual techniques are used to create a well-composed film.<br><br>The film makes excellent use of both a-roll and b-roll footage. | Some different shot styles, lighting, and visual techniques are used in the film.<br><br>The film uses both a-roll and b-roll footage. | The film's look is basic and unengaging to the audience.<br><br>The film does not use a-roll and b-roll footage in a thoughtful way. |
| **Audio** | High-quality audio of interviews and narrations are clear and easy to understand.<br><br>The score and additional audio enhance the viewing experience and draw the audience into the film. | Audio of interviews and narrations can be heard and understood by the audience.<br><br>The score and additional audio are used to enhance the film. | Audio recordings are low-quality and distracting.<br><br>The score and additional audio detract from the film. |
| **Editing** | Deliberate editing decisions move the film forward from beginning to end.<br><br>The film features seamless integration of transitions, credits, and thoughtful cuts. | Some editing decisions help move the film along.<br><br>The film features some transitions, credits, and cuts. | Poor editing leaves the film feeling slow or hard to understand.<br><br>The film features few or no transitions, credits, or cuts. |

**FIGURE 6.1:** *Documentary rubric.*

*Visit **go.SolutionTree.com/technology** for a free reproducible version of this figure.*

better life choices. That's who these filmmakers are, what these filmmakers do, and why our students need to be making (short) documentary films.

Before students begin their projects, they first need to understand the characteristics and components of a well-made documentary short film. Providing model documentary shorts, such as the following, for students to evaluate with the documentary rubric (figure 6.1, page 107) is a great way to clarify your expectations for students' final products and what success can look like on this project.

- **StoryMaker (www.story-maker.org):** This is a free learning platform developed by PBS NewsHour Student Reporting Labs to build the next generation of media creators. In addition to a library of student-created documentary shorts and news stories, StoryMaker features a personalized educator dashboard with lesson plans, classroom activities, and media-making challenges.
- **"8 Ways to Teach With Short Documentary Films From the Times" (https://tinyurl.com/ch7eprat):** This article from *The New York Times* presents eight ideas for teaching short documentary filmmaking, including several films to watch, discussion questions, and activities for each idea.
- **The Global Oneness Project (www.globalonenessproject.org):** This site hosts short documentary films and student contests that highlight global communities, cultures, and environmental issues. Accompanying lesson plans encourage students to reflect through writing and broaden their perspectives and worldviews.

## The Project

Students will form film crews with assigned roles to collaboratively create a documentary short film in this digital project. The documentary planning page shown in figure 6.2 outlines the steps students in my class follow to successfully complete this digital project.

Just as you've seen for the podcast project (chapter 4, page 61) and video 101 film school (chapter 5, page 77), there are three stages of video production: (1) preproduction, (2) production, and (3) postproduction. Your student film crews will progress through these project stages at their own pace, so while you'll want to revisit chapter 5's film concepts, production roles, and so on, you'll also want to allot time during class and outside of school hours for students to work on their documentary short films wherever they are in the process.

### *Preproduction*

During preproduction, each film crew will collectively decide on their documentary topic and complete the subsequent steps necessary to begin production. To help facilitate the successful completion of all preproduction tasks and ensure a fair distribution of work among team members, I require my film crews to assign each of these individual tasks to one or two students.

- Write the treatment.
- Pitch the film.
- Conduct research.
- Draft interview questions.
- Complete shot list and editing organizer.

| **Filmmakers:** | **Film Title and Topic:** |
|---|---|
| **Preproduction** ||
| Step 1: Brainstorm ideas for the film and select a topic or subject. <br> Topic or subject: _____ <br> Step 2: Write a treatment for the film and pitch the project. <br> Step 3: Research information, images, and interesting facts to include in the film. <br> Step 4: Complete the shot list and editing organizer. ||
| **Production:** ||
| Step 5: Shoot primary (a-roll) and secondary (b-roll) footage. <br> Step 6: Conduct interviews. <br> Step 7: Record additional audio, including narration and sound effects. ||
| **Postproduction** ||
| Step 8: Edit the film: video, still images, narration, music, transitions, effects, and credits. <br> Step 9: Screen the rough cut for the teacher and at least two critical friends. We will each give you a score using the rubric and a Critical Friend Feedback Form. Continue editing as needed. <br> Step 10: Present the final product during the film festival. <br> Step 11: Publish the film online and complete an After-Project Reflection. ||

**FIGURE 6.2:** Documentary planning.

*Visit* **go.SolutionTree.com/technology** *for a free reproducible version of this figure.*

Your film crews are ready to begin the preproduction process once they have assigned these tasks strategically and fairly to their members.

### Step 1: Brainstorm Ideas for the Film and Select a Topic

The documentary short films my students create all have run times of less than five minutes, which is a short window to make a strong case or tell a complete story. So, during our initial lesson, we watch two documentaries that are both shorter than five minutes and evaluate them together using this project's rubric (figure 6.1, page 107). Then, I help my students organize themselves into film crews, and they begin brainstorming ideas for their own films.

Documentaries typically either focus on a topic (climate change, gun violence, and so on) or a subject (a man who owns tigers, cheerleaders in southern U.S. states, and so on). My students use the documentary topic selection page featured in figure 6.3 (page 110) to select a subject the whole team is interested in or a topic they want to investigate, elevate, or propose solutions for in their films. Film crews also discuss who their target audience should be, the themes they want to explore and communicate, and their purpose in making their films (inform others, create change, and so on).

I tell my students to think broadly when selecting a topic to explore and then zero in on a narrow focus for their film. For example, a documentary crew once decided they wanted to make a film about art. After discussing it further, they narrowed their focus to art created by immigrants, then art created by immigrant children, and finally, they decided to focus their film on their own visual and musical artistic works.

**Brainstorm**

1. What topic would you be most excited to explore in your film? Explain why.

2. Who would be the intended audience for your film? Explain why.

3. What themes would you like to explore and communicate in your film?

4. What would be your purpose in making this film (to inform others, raise awareness, or create change)? How would you achieve that purpose?

5. Who would you need to interview for your documentary, and what would you want to ask them?

**FIGURE 6.3:** *Documentary topic selection.*
*Visit **go.SolutionTree.com/technology** for a free reproducible version of this figure.*

Scan the QR code to check out their documentary short film, *The Art of Immigrant Kids*.

I tell my film crews to think of selecting a topic together like choosing a single meal to share in the food court at the mall (if malls still exist when this book comes out). First, you wander around a bit, then you pick a restaurant you're all in the mood for, and then you can talk about ordering something specific off the menu. Once a team identifies a general topic they want to study and a specific focus for their investigation, then they're ready to go out and find a story to tell.

## Step 2: Write a Treatment for the Film and Pitch the Project

As defined in chapter 5 (page 77), a film treatment is a written summary that provides an overview of the film project. In addition to the topic, audience, theme, and purpose, the documentary treatment featured in figure 6.4 includes a logline for the film and a basic outline of its story arc (Act 1, Act 2, and Act 3).

| Filmmakers: | Logline: |
|---|---|
| Topic: | Act 1: |
| Audience: | Act 2: |
| Theme (the message): | Act 3: |

**FIGURE 6.4:** *Documentary treatment.*

*Visit* **go.SolutionTree.com/technology** *for a free reproducible version of this figure.*

Each team selects one spokesperson to pitch their film concept to me once their treatment is complete. During these five-minute sessions, I like to ask quick, probing questions of the whole team to clarify any confusion I might have and determine how interested everyone really is in the chosen topic or subject. Afterward, I fill out a "Critical Friend Feedback Form" (see page 157 in the appendix), letting them know what I liked about their film pitch, what I still wonder about, and one suggestion I have for the group. Sometimes, I invite guests like our school's librarian or media specialist or local filmmakers to conduct these pitching sessions with me, upping the ante for my presenting students and providing them with further feedback. If I determine their treatment needs more work, then the students go back and rework their concept; however, if a team has a solid concept they are committed to bringing to the screen, then their project gets the green light, and they move on to step 3.

### Step 3: Research Information, Images, and Interesting Facts to Include in the Film

The goal of the research process is for students to collect quantitative (measurable and numbers-based) and qualitative (categorical and language-based) data that underlie the importance and relevance of their documentaries. Students' research will be used to draft narration for the film, determine a- and b-roll shot lists, and inform editing decisions in postproduction. As students gather facts and figures in a digital document, make sure they also record the bibliographical information as they go so it's easy to cite their sources in the end credits of their films. Revisit chapter 1 (page 13) for resources and lesson ideas for teaching media literacy to students and finding credible, reliable sources online.

As with previous projects in this book, have your students begin by completing the "Five Fascinating Facts Form" (page 156 in the appendix) about their topic or subject. Also, since so much of the information presented in a documentary comes from interviews conducted with a variety of individuals, your film crews must use their research to narrow their search for qualified and compelling interview subjects. Students need to select individuals who are *local* and accessible for interviews, and they should look to their own communities for the expertise and experience needed to speak thoughtfully about issues relevant to their lives. Figure 6.5 shows an example of the template I provide my students for their initial emails to potential interviewees.

---

Hi [name],

My name is [your name], and I am a sixth-grade student at Meadowlark Elementary. My classmates and I are producing a short documentary film about [your topic], and we would like to interview you for our project. If you are willing to be interviewed by us, please contact our teacher at [email address] or [phone number].

Sincerely,

[Your name]

---

**FIGURE 6.5:** Short film interview request message.

To ensure students' safety, the initial email and all further communications should be run through your email and telephone. The only exception to this rule is if the interview subject is a student's friend, family member, or trusted adult in our school community that they invite in person to be in their film. Even then, you should be copied on any subsequent emails and included in any project-related text conversations. Once students know who they want to interview, they need their subject's permission to capture their conversation on film. There are countless release forms to choose from online, but as shown in figure 4.5 (page 69) for podcast projects, my favorite interview release form is on the Library of Congress website.

Film crews also need to decide what kind of interviews they want to conduct. There are five main types of interviews seen in documentary films.

1. **Formal:** Only the interview subject is seen or heard. The interviewer is off camera, their questions usually aren't heard, and the focus is on the subject's response.
2. **Journalistic:** Both the interviewer and subject are together in the same camera frame, and the audience typically hears both the questions and the responses.
3. **News magazine:** The interviewer and subject face each other, with one camera on the interviewer and another on the subject.
4. **Action:** The subject is seen and interviewed in action (for example, playing their musical instrument or cooking a delicious meal while being interviewed).
5. **Vox pop:** Interview everyday people on the street to get a sense of what they know or think about the documentary topic or subject.

Here are a few guiding questions film crews can discuss to determine which interview styles will best meet the needs of their documentary.

1. How many experts or individuals do we want to hear from?
2. Will seeing or hearing our interviewer help us tell this story?
3. Do we want the camera to move during the interviews?
4. Does the audience need to see our subject in action, or are their words and perspective enough to tell the story?

Student documentary sets are abuzz just before an interview begins. The grip is positioning tripods and rigging lights. The director and cinematographer are preparing the interview subject, sitting them down strategically within their thoughtfully crafted shot. The sound designer is checking audio levels and recording at least thirty seconds of ambient sound. It's fun, it's exciting—and none of it will matter if the interview questions aren't on point.

The first rule of writing high-quality questions is to keep them open-ended. Nothing slows down an interview faster than asking a question with a yes-or-no answer. Thankfully, it's easy to transform a yes-or-no question into an open-ended one. For example, instead of asking, "Did you enjoy school today?" you can ask, "What were some things you learned at school today?" Another way to avoid a one-word answer is to have students phrase questions that will elicit a thorough response.

- "Tell me about . . ."
- "Explain why . . ."
- "How did you . . ."
- "Describe for us . . ."

Because my students' films are no longer than five minutes, I limit my filmmakers to three to five well-written questions per interview subject, with the understanding that follow-up questions will likely flow naturally during their conversations. Each team turns in their written questions for review, and I conference with students whose questions need to be revised. After any necessary changes are made, we send their questions to the interviewees for final approval.

### Step 4: Complete the Shot List and Editing Organizer

Documentary filmmaking is a fluid art form, because stories constantly evolve and can head off in new directions from one interview to the next. However, by creating a shot list that outlines the still images and video footage students deem necessary for their documentary, they can better manage the production flow before it begins. The documentary shot list and editing organizer shown in figure 6.6 allows students to identify the critical elements they need to capture for their films: visuals, audio, and text or scripted narration.

The interviews designated as a-roll footage on students' shot lists will drive most video, audio, and script or narration decisions made throughout the process. B-roll footage for a short documentary might include landscape and scenery, shots of your students' subject interacting with elements within a space, establishing shots, and backgrounds. Still, I encourage my students to storyboard shots they have in mind within the boxes in figure 6.6 and organize their interviews with the following three-act structure in mind.

- **Act 1:** Establish your characters, setting, and topic or subject.
- **Act 2:** Keep your audience engaged with information, personal narratives, and building action.
- **Act 3:** Wrap up with a conclusion or resolution.

With a story arc and shared vision of their film in hand, I now send my filmmakers out to scout shooting locations. Ninety percent of the locations where my students film are in our school: classrooms, hallways, playgrounds, the library, and so on. Young filmmakers are looking for locations where they can capture high-quality video and audio (places that have good lighting and a quiet environment) and create compelling sets for interviews; most importantly, they should select locations that *best serve the story*. Students often ask me what I mean by that. For example, one of my crews filmed a short documentary about the teachers and paraprofessionals in our school who work with our special education students. What locations would help tell their story? Here's a sentence frame I use to help my creators pick the right locations for their films.

*Our film is about _____. So, filming in _____ will help us tell our story because _____.*

As a reminder, students filming in school must secure permission to shoot in their scouted locations—including specific times and dates—from school administrators and the adult who is most responsible for each space. Prior to filming, they also need to confirm that the location is still available and profusely thank whoever is allowing them to film there. When my students film at off-site locations before or after school, they again need to secure the proper permissions, as well as provide me with a detailed travel plan to and from their sets and the parents, caregivers, or other responsible adults who will be supervising and supporting them during their shoot.

Audio in a documentary film includes dialogue from interviews or captured conversations, narration, music, sound effects, and ambient noise. While most of the dialogue and ambient noise recorded during filming is captured spontaneously in the moment, students can use the documentary shot list and editing organizer (figure 6.6) to preplan where in the flow of their story important narration and musical cues should be inserted.

| A-Roll Footage (Interviews and Action): | B-Roll Footage: |
|---|---|
| Interviews and shots you need in your film. | Extra footage and shots that would be nice to have. |
| 1. | 6. |
| 2. | 7. |
| 3. | 8. |
| 4. | 9. |
| 5. | 10. |

| Visuals | Audio | Script and Narration |
|---|---|---|
|  |  |  |
|  |  |  |
|  |  |  |
|  |  |  |

**FIGURE 6.6** *Documentary shot list and editing organizer.*

Visit **go.SolutionTree.com/technology** *for a free reproducible version of this figure.*

## Production

Your students are finally ready to begin filming. They now need access to whatever film equipment you have available. Remember, the only two must-have pieces of equipment each film crew will need are a camera and microphone, both of which are included with your students' laptops or mobile devices, but you can review the guidance in chapter 5 (page 77) for a refresher of your options. Always remember that brilliant films are often made better by sticking with the simplest tools. For example, here are three excellent documentary short films shot entirely on smartphones.

1. A Woman's Epic Journey to Climb 7 Mountains (https://youtu.be/wMqu-nRM-Uc)
2. The Painter of Jalouzi (https://youtu.be/Eyr9NwyszNY)
3. Syria: Songs of Defiance (https://youtu.be/VnvPXspjLtU)

Before a crew starts filming, each student needs to clearly identify and articulate their assigned production role. The most typical roles on a documentary short film crew are director, cinematographer (visuals), sound designer (audio), and grip (equipment). To increase efficiency and add some fun on set, make sure film crews also revisit the list of common filmmaking production cues from chapter 5. Encourage them to use industry terms, such as *quiet on set*, *camera rolling*, *roll sound*, *action*, and *cut*. Finally, review the following information with students.

- Principles of cinematography (rule of thirds, depth of field, and the twelve shot styles)
- Location, lighting, and sound
- Copyright and fair use

### Step 5: Shoot Primary (A-Roll) and Secondary (B-Roll) Footage

The goal of any film shoot is to capture all the visuals needed to tell a particular story. However, to score a three for visuals on our rubric, student filmmakers should shoot a-roll and b-roll footage using a variety of shot styles, lighting, and visual techniques to create a well-composed film. *A-roll* footage is the primary video captured for a film; in a documentary, a-roll includes all interviews and main action shots that are necessary to tell the story. *B-roll* footage is secondary video or still images that help illustrate the story or add depth and context to the film. For your students' documentaries, b-roll footage might include landscape and scenery, insert shots of elements within a space, establishing shots, and backgrounds.

The audience should be able to turn off the sound and still enjoy the beautifully framed shots and interviews, and the message of the documentary should resonate through its visuals. Students should check the following three things before pressing record.

1. The background and set are clean and uncluttered.
2. The subject is lit in a lovely way.
3. The camera angle draws the viewer into the conversation.

After that, it's "Quiet on set—lights . . . camera . . . *action!*"

Here are my five tips for keeping things cool, calm, and collected throughout your documentary production.

1. Maintain an updated sign-out sheet for your digital equipment (refer to figure 5.14, page 98).
2. As video is shot and captured on phones or memory cards, provide each team with a digital project folder on their computer for storing all their footage and any other images, audio, and so on, needed for their video. Create three subfolders—video,

audio, and other media—within each project folder so filmmakers can stay organized and save time when they get to postproduction (see "Digital Tools and Technology Tips," page 25 in chapter 1).
3. Students can only shoot at locations they have scouted ahead of time.
4. Students can shoot outside of school hours and manage those logistics themselves. However, if students are filming during school, only one group can shoot outside of the classroom at a time. I post a simple shooting calendar where students can sign up for specific dates, times, and locations in the school.
5. Students must shoot at least one safety (additional take) for each critical shot.

### Step 6: Conduct Interviews

People often get nervous or tighten up once they are in front of a camera, including adults—that's why it is important for interviewers to ease their subjects into the conversation. I encourage my students to begin their interviews with factual, straightforward questions and save the more personal or emotionally loaded material for later in the interview when their subject has had time to get more comfortable. Students should always finish interviews by asking their subjects, "Is there anything else you want to add or anything we forgot to cover?" And, of course, no interview is ever complete until the interviewer thanks their guest for their time and participation.

Like adult filmmakers, students are likely to come into their projects already knowing what they want to say and the point they want to make. Remind your young documentarians to stay open to changing their minds or shifting their perspectives based on what they learn during their interviews. As I said before, documentarians are dedicated to asking and answering their own questions; I love reminding my students that the root of the word *question* is *quest*. As documentarians, that's what you're on—a journey of discovery and purpose toward an unknown destination. If students come into this project with a fixed ending in mind, they're limiting their opportunities for learning and growth along the way.

### Step 7: Record Additional Audio, Including Narration and Sound Effects

There's a reason why a director's first words before filming are *quiet on set*. No matter how pretty or professional a documentary might look, bad audio can ruin the whole thing. Throughout a shoot, the sound designer needs to always have their headphones on, listening to the audio being captured for any noises that might distract or impede the audience from hearing the speech or actions. For best results, students should place a lavalier mic on anyone speaking and connect them to their own laptop, smartphone, or other audio recording device. Finally, if sounds on set can be controlled or eliminated (think air conditioners, fans, and machines that buzz or hum), it's the sound designer's job to do so. However, if noises on set are being caused by forces beyond your students' control (such as wind, traffic, or a passing plane), then the crew will either need to wait or relocate before filming.

The following are four useful tips for recording high-quality audio.
1. Eliminate as much background noise as possible before filming.
2. Record thirty seconds of ambient sound to lay over any gaps or b-roll footage in postproduction.

3. Use external mics whenever possible.
4. Record voiceover narration and sound effects in a small, silent room to avoid echoes and ambient sounds.

## Postproduction

Now that all the visual and auditory elements of your students' films have been collected, it's time to combine them into a well-told story and a short, cohesive film. Just as in production, each film crew member should be assigned a clearly defined postproduction role (refer to chapter 5, page 77, for a refresher on this process). The postproduction roles I always assign my students are the director (continuing in this role from production), editor, sound editor, and assistant editor. While the three editors have individual responsibilities, the director collaborates with all three throughout postproduction to connect their collective vision for their documentary short film.

### Step 8: Edit the Film

Throughout production, each film crew has deposited the video, audio, and other media files they've collected into their digital project folder. Now that production is complete, it is the assistant editor's job to review all the media files with the director and catalog everything the crew has collected. First, I have my students create three digital folders titled Act 1, Act 2, and Act 3. Working with the director, the assistant editor labels each media file according to its act and a defining characteristic of the clip before sorting it into the appropriate folder (such as *Act 1—Ismail introduces himself; Act 3—b-roll walking into a house*). This is also a great opportunity to weed out and delete any video or audio files from production that the crew knows they won't want to use in the final film; however, if there is even a chance that your students may want to include a clip or piece of audio in their edit, make sure they *don't delete it*! I've seen students cry when they realized they deleted a simple reaction shot or quiet comment that would have tied their whole film together. If this happens, make sure to check for a deleted items folder in the application your students are using. Many editing apps keep deleted content recoverable for a short time.

Once sorted, the assistant editor's final job is to import all media files into whatever video editing software they will be using. From there, the editor can drag those files onto the timeline and begin to craft the story. Thankfully, after plotting out their documentaries in preproduction and fleshing out their films during production, the director and editor usually enter this stage with a clear understanding of how these pieces should all fit together.

Again, the editor's true work is less in telling the story than it is in *crafting* the story. The editor must painstakingly examine the impact a fraction of a second of video might have on the film's overall flow. Editing can be tedious, meticulous work, so make sure each film crew picks the right student for the job. Per my guidance in chapter 5, look for the students who can't stand to color outside the lines, use a ruler to rip a piece of paper, and lean in real close when they're cutting with scissors—these students are your editors.

Congratulations! At this point, your students' film clips have been edited together, and the puzzle pieces all fit perfectly. Your editor has added titles, credits, and text to the timeline, and their rough cut has the look of a finished product. However, we enjoy films with both our eyes and our ears, so it's now time for the sound editor to add the final audiological flourishes to the film. First, they ensure the audio captured along with the video footage is high-quality and matches the on-screen lip movement; if there are any issues, the sound editor works with the director and editor to determine whether clips need to be replaced or if audio needs to be rerecorded. Next, if additional audio needs to be captured (sound effects, voiceover narration, and so on), the sound editor works with the director to record it and import it for the editor to weave into the film. Finally, the sound editor is responsible for downloading and importing music options for the editor (check out the open-source music options in "Edit the Fifteen-Second Film," page 100 in chapter 5).

Most students naturally understand when a piece of music is tonally and thematically a nice match for their film. Still, I love facilitating conversations about music for film crews by scoring their works with my own horrible musical selections (think carnival music or a funeral dirge). By playfully discussing the kinds of music that don't serve their film, students can more easily articulate the musical elements that would connect with audiences and elevate their documentaries.

### Step 9: Screen the Rough Cut for the Teacher and at Least Two Critical Friends

For this project, screen each film's rough cut on your computer with two different film crews: (1) the students who shot the film and (2) another crew to review it. Watch the film together and then discuss it using the documentary rubric (figure 6.1, page 107) and "Critical Friend Feedback Form" (page 157 in the appendix). This way, you are providing valuable feedback to the filmmakers whose short you just enjoyed, and you're also sending the crew of reviewers back to work with greater insights and ideas for revising their own films.

### Step 10: Present the Final Product During the Film Festival

While many teachers assign project deadlines or due dates, I prefer to provide my film crews with a release date by which they must finish their films to premier at our very own film festival.

This step is not a requirement, and you are welcome to disregard the rest of this paragraph. However, after all the hard work you and your students put into this project, a public exhibition and celebration of their creative achievement is certainly deserved and always a hit. It can be as simple as an afternoon or evening screening of your students' films for friends and families at school. Or, depending on where you are, there may also be film festivals organized by outside organizations that your students can submit their films to. For example, here in Utah, we have the Tumbleweeds Film Festival (https://tumbleweedskids.org), hosted by the Utah Film Center and Utah Education Network, which features a student film competition, activities, and workshops for children of all ages. Either way, I encourage your students to watch their short films on the big screen in front of a live audience, even if it's just in the school cafeteria or auditorium—it's something they'll never forget.

### Step 11: Publish the Film Online and Complete an After-Project Reflection

Whether posting your students' documentaries on your school's learning management system or an online video-sharing platform, you'll want to discuss how broadly your crews want their work distributed and how they hope to reach their target audience. As I've said, my students publish their video projects on our class's YouTube channel, @9thEvermore, because they want their work accessible to other students just like them—that's who they are creating content for. However, most often, my film crews have chosen to post their documentaries privately because they want to determine exactly who gets to watch them. This is a team decision that every film crew makes together, and I always look forward to facilitating that conversation.

As always, before your digital content creators move on to their next project, have them reflect on their filmmaking experience by completing an "After-Project Reflection Form" (page 158 in the appendix).

## Conclusion

Film crews, expensive equipment, location scouting, interview release forms—let's be honest, creating documentary short films with students is a lot. I'm a big fan of this digital project because I've seen its positive, lasting effects on my students, but it's definitely not for the faint of heart.

Let's revisit our objective for this project: *I will empower my students' voices by teaching them to share information, raise awareness, and advocate for positive change through film.* This project is all about teaching students to share with others the things they personally value or find interesting. If you still want your students to create digital projects that combine sights with sounds but require less time and coordination than documentary films, here are a few related project ideas to consider.

- Film a thirty- to sixty-second public service announcement on your chosen topic. This provides students with preproduction, production, and postproduction experience but with a much simpler product and shorter timeline.

- Create a slideshow presentation on your topic with audio recorded over each slide. Students would still need to edit media together to tell a compelling story, learn to record narration, and possibly incorporate music and sound effects into their projects, but they can do so without coordinating a film shoot or capturing video in the field.

- Record an interview with an expert on your chosen topic. Conducting an effective interview is perhaps the most valuable learning experience in this project, and cutting everything from the production besides the interview would focus all attention on the importance of that conversation.

# CHAPTER 7
# Narrative Short Films

**PROJECT OBJECTIVE**

I will empower my students' voices by teaching them to share their stories and messages with an online audience.

**Definition of *Film***

**noun**
A motion picture; a movie.

**verb**
Capture on film as part of a series of moving images; make a movie of (a story or event).

—*Oxford English Dictionary Online*

## CREATORS AT WORK

"*No!* There's no way you're climbing on the school's roof for that shot!"

"But, Captain," Mohammed said, exasperated, and pointed down at the playground pavement, "That's the only way to let the audience know our main character's been transported to the roof. We *need* a shot looking down at the ground from his point-of-view up there!"

This was the last shot of the day. Mohammed and his crew had been filming for two hours after school on a gray winter day. Their short horror film, *Fly*, told the story of a child who gets a job as an after-school sweeper, and during his first shift, he's haunted by the ghost of a student who died in the school. Terrifyingly transported from one location in the building to the next, the sweeper quickly learns two things about this vengeful spirit: (1) it loves music and (2) it wants to fly.

I looked at Mohammed's lead actor on this project, Tau, and said, "Tau's not going on the roof."

"But he wouldn't go alone. Issa would go up to film him, too!"

Issa, the cinematographer, was lying on the ground with my iPhone, framing Tau in a low-angle shot with nothing behind him except the sky so it would appear to the audience as if he were standing precariously on the ledge of our school's extremely tall, two-story roof. Issa looked up just long enough to say, "I ain't going up there."

Before Mohammed could argue with his friend, I quickly added, "You don't even need that shot. You've got this one from below."

Mohammed squeezed his head between his palms. "It won't work! The only way for the audience to know he's on the roof is for us to see him *on the roof*. On the narrative film rubric**,** it says we need a variety of shot styles, right? Here's our low-angle shot, and now we need our high-angle shot!" If nothing else, he was right about the rubric (see figure 7.1).

"Well, I can't send any kids up on the roof, so that's that," I answered.

Mohammed turned to me with an idea. "Captain, could *you* go on the roof?"

I thought about squashing this thought like a bug, but it was getting late, and I needed to pick up my daughter from daycare.

"I absolutely can. What do you want me to do?"

And that's how I ended up on the roof of Meadowlark Elementary, slipping and sliding in the snow on my way to the ledge, with just a thigh-high wall between me and a sudden drop. I removed my shoes and set them on the wall (Tau and I wore the same super-hip sneakers), toes pointed out into space, and captured ten seconds of an insert shot pointed straight down at the ground below.

When the boys premiered their short film in class, the students gasped when they saw Tau wobbling on the roof, clearly this close to falling. "You got to go on the roof?!" one girl asked loudly.

"Nah," Mohammed said. "We sent Captain up there."

"Then how come it looks like Tau's on the roof?"

Before he could answer, Issa whispered, "Movie magic!"

 Scan the QR code and decide for yourself whether the boys pulled off their magic trick.

**I DON'T KNOW ABOUT** you, but I used to make movies with my friends when I was a kid, lugging my dad's heavy VHS camcorder into the mountains to shoot fight scenes among the trees. Of all the projects in this book, this is the one students will most likely do just for fun outside of school. Right now, everywhere in the world, there are bleary-eyed students in classrooms who stayed up way past their bedtime watching shows or movies on their phones, and they would give anything to learn how to create keep-you-up-at-night content, too. I say it's time we teach them, and while we're at it, channel that interest into mastering content and empowering our students to share their stories with audiences.

Narrative films tell stories—most often fictional—in a condensed format, typically ranging from a few minutes to twenty minutes in length. Unlike feature-length films, which require substantial resources and time commitments, these films offer a unique avenue for our young creators to tell powerful stories with limited resources and time constraints. These films encompass a wide scope of genres, including thought-provoking dramas, lighthearted comedies, the horror movies my students love most, and even experimental works of art. Narrative short films make the perfect project for most English language arts classrooms and can be adapted to support standard mastery in social studies, foreign language courses, and other content areas. In shooting narrative short films, students develop a deep understanding of effective visual storytelling techniques because they distill their ideas into succinct narrative arcs that follow a three-act structure

|  | **3** | **2** | **1** |
|---|---|---|---|
| **Content** | The film shares an interesting story or message that moves the audience's thoughts or actions. | The film tells a story or communicates a message to the audience. | The film's story or message is unclear. |
| **Narrative Structure** | The film has an excellent hook that engages the audience. There is a clear beginning, middle, and end to the film. | The film has a good hook for the audience. There is some sense of a beginning, middle, and end to the film. | The film lacks an organized structure. |
| **Visuals** | A variety of shot styles, lighting, and visual techniques create a well-composed film. The film makes excellent use of both a-roll and b-roll footage. | The film uses some different shot styles, lighting, and visual techniques. The film makes use of both a-roll and b-roll footage. | The film's look is basic and unengaging to the audience. The film does not use a-roll and b-roll footage in a thoughtful way. |
| **Audio** | High-quality audio and narrations are clear and easy to understand. The score and additional audio enhance the viewing experience and draw the audience into the film. | Audio and narrations can be heard and understood by the audience. The score and additional audio are used to enhance the film. | Audio recordings are low-quality and distracting. The score and additional audio detract from the film. |
| **Editing** | Deliberate editing decisions move the film forward from beginning to end. Seamless integration of transitions, credits, and thoughtful cuts are used in the film. | Some editing decisions help move the film along. Transitions, credits, and cuts are used in the film. | Poor editing leaves the film feeling slow or hard to understand. Few or no transitions, credits, or cuts are used in the film. |

**FIGURE 7.1:** *Narrative film rubric.*

*Visit* ***go.SolutionTree.com/technology*** *for a free reproducible version of this figure.*

(beginning, middle, and end), often leaving their audiences with profound and lasting impressions. These filmmaking projects are concise and can be used to support learning in any content area. They provide young creators with a meaningful outlet for their creativity and foster self-expression and empathy—and above all else, they're super fun!

Before students begin their projects, they must first understand the characteristics and components of a well-made narrative short film. Providing model narrative shorts, such as the following, for students to evaluate using the narrative film rubric (figure 7.1, page 123) is a great way to clarify your expectations for your students' final products and what success can look like on this project.

- **The Utah Film Center (https://utahfilmcenter.org/education/free-films-for-teachers):** I shared this resource in chapter 5 (page 77), and I want to again highlight their site as a remarkable repository of films, short films, and public service announcements that include study guides and are available to stream for free in the classroom.
- **Film School Shorts (https://utah.pbslearningmedia.org/collection/filmschoolshorts):** This site showcases some of the best shorts from film schools across the United States, including New York University; University of California, Los Angeles; and Columbia University. These shorts were all made by rising filmmakers still mastering their craft and have premiered at prestigious film festivals like Sundance, Cannes, and South by Southwest (SXSW). This collection from PBS Learning Media features nine videos intended for students in grades 6–12.
- **The National Film Board of Canada (www.nfb.ca/education/educational-playlists):** This resource provides curated educational playlists of films selected based on their curriculum connections and that address important historical or current global issues. Many of the films also come with study guides and minilessons with age recommendations, key vocabulary, essential questions, and classroom activities to connect the films' themes to their own lived experiences.

## The Project

In this digital project, students will form film crews with assigned roles to collaboratively create a narrative short film. The narrative film planning page (figure 7.2) outlines the steps my class follows to successfully complete this digital project.

Some steps take one class session to complete, and others can take weeks. As expected based on previous projects, there are three stages of video production: (1) preproduction, (2) production, (3) postproduction. Your student film crews will progress through these stages at their own pace, so while you'll want to revisit film concepts, production roles, and so on as a whole class (see chapter 5, page 77), you will also want to allot time during class and outside of school hours for students to work on their narrative films wherever they are in the process.

Please note that if you've already read the chapter 6 (page 105) project for making a documentary short film, you will notice that many (though not all) of the steps and the directions in this chapter match those of the documentary project. This is by design. While narrative films and documentaries have many shared elements, and their shared steps and guidance reflect this, there are still critical differences that make these distinct projects with distinct outcomes.

| **Filmmakers:** | **Film Title and Topic:** |
|---|---|
| **Preproduction** ||
| Step 1: Complete the treatment for the script. ||
| Step 2: Draft the script. ||
| Step 3: Select a script as a crew and pitch the film. ||
| Step 4: Create storyboards for the film. ||
| **Production** ||
| Step 5: Shoot primary (a-roll) and secondary (b-roll) footage. ||
| Step 6: Record additional audio, including narration and sound effects. ||
| **Postproduction** ||
| Step 7: Edit the film: video, still images, narration, music, transitions, effects, and credits. ||
| Step 8: Screen the rough cut for the teacher and at least two critical friends. We will each give you a score with the rubric and a Critical Friend Feedback Form. Continue editing as needed. ||
| Step 9: Present the final product during the film festival. ||
| Step 10: Publish the film online and complete an After-Project Reflection. ||

**FIGURE 7.2:** Narrative film planning.

Visit **go.SolutionTree.com/technology** for a free reproducible version of this figure.

## Preproduction

During preproduction, each film crew will decide together what story they want to tell and complete the subsequent steps necessary to begin production. Once a script is selected by the crew to film, they must assign each of these individual tasks to one or two students.

- Revise and finalize the script.
- Complete a narrative film pitch sheet.
- Pitch the film.
- Create storyboards.

### Step 1: Complete the Treatment for the Script

The narrative short films my students create all have run times of less than five minutes, which is a short window to tell a complete story. So, during the initial lesson, we watch two model narrative short films that are also shorter than five minutes, evaluating them together using this project's rubric (figure 7.1, page 123). I also have my students fill out a narrative short film treatment as shown in figure 7.3 (page 126) for each model film so they can see how each film's story arc includes a conflict, plot events, and resolution. As you explore the catalog of short films available in the recommended online resources, you will notice that many are animated. Although my students don't make animated films in our class, I often still include them as models because they capture the rubric's critical elements, and upper-elementary students like mine really enjoy them.

| Characters: | Setting: |
|---|---|//

| Introduction and Conflict: |
|---|

| Plot Events: |
|---|

| Climax: |
|---|

| Resolution: |
|---|

| Genre: | Theme: | Logline: |
|---|---|---|

**FIGURE 7.3:** *Narrative short film treatment.*

*Visit* **go.SolutionTree.com/technology** *for a free reproducible version of this figure.*

Next, students start brainstorming ideas and writing treatments for their films. As we defined in chapter 5 (page 77), a film treatment is a written summary that provides an overview of the film project. At this step, there are two options: (1) students form film crews and develop their treatments together, or (2) each student writes their own treatment and script, and then, as a film crew, they select the script they are all most excited to shoot. I've tried this project both ways, and my filmmakers have always had greater success with the second option. So, that's how I've designed the planning page for this project, and I would have my students outline their own stories on the narrative short film treatment form as an independent writing assignment.

### *Step 2: Draft the Script*

During film school (see chapter 5, page 77), students learned the fundamentals of writing a script using the short film screenplay template (refer to figure 5.7, page 89) as their guide. Again, your students can write their scripts using whatever format *you* are most comfortable with, including a short story format or reader's theater. As I said before, however, it's so fun writing a screenplay like the pros.

### *Step 3: Select a Script as a Crew and Pitch the Film*

I let my students divide themselves into film crews of no more than four, with the understanding that, if necessary, they can ask students from other crews to act in their short films (usually as background extras). After the crews are formed, each member reads their own screenplay draft aloud to their teammates. Following each reading, the other film crew members must share at least one thing they appreciate about the script. Once all crew members have presented, the team must decide which script they will film together for this project, keeping in mind that they can always film their own or another script for fun in the future.

Sometimes, it's an easy pick—there's one screenplay that's so amazing that everyone is on board with filming it. Other times, not so much; everyone wants their own script to be chosen, or there's one member of a film crew who is so bummed by the team's decision that they threaten not to participate. Teachers put structures in place to prevent issues like these from occurring during any collaborative group project. For this step in creating a short film, I have three rules that help keep the drama to a minimum.

1. Scripts must be nominated for selection, and you cannot nominate your own.
2. The majority rules. If there is a tie between two scripts, you must revisit each screenplay and respectfully discuss the pros and cons of shooting either one before you can take another vote.
3. Any member of the film crew can propose script revisions, but they must be agreed on by the majority of the team.

Once the team selects their screenplay, the writer revises and edits the script with any feedback they've received from their teammates. Each film crew then selects one spokesperson to pitch their film concept to me. Ahead of the pitch, each crew fills out a narrative film pitch sheet (figure 7.4, page 128) to help solidify their collective understanding of the film's themes, purpose, intended audience, and technical requirements.

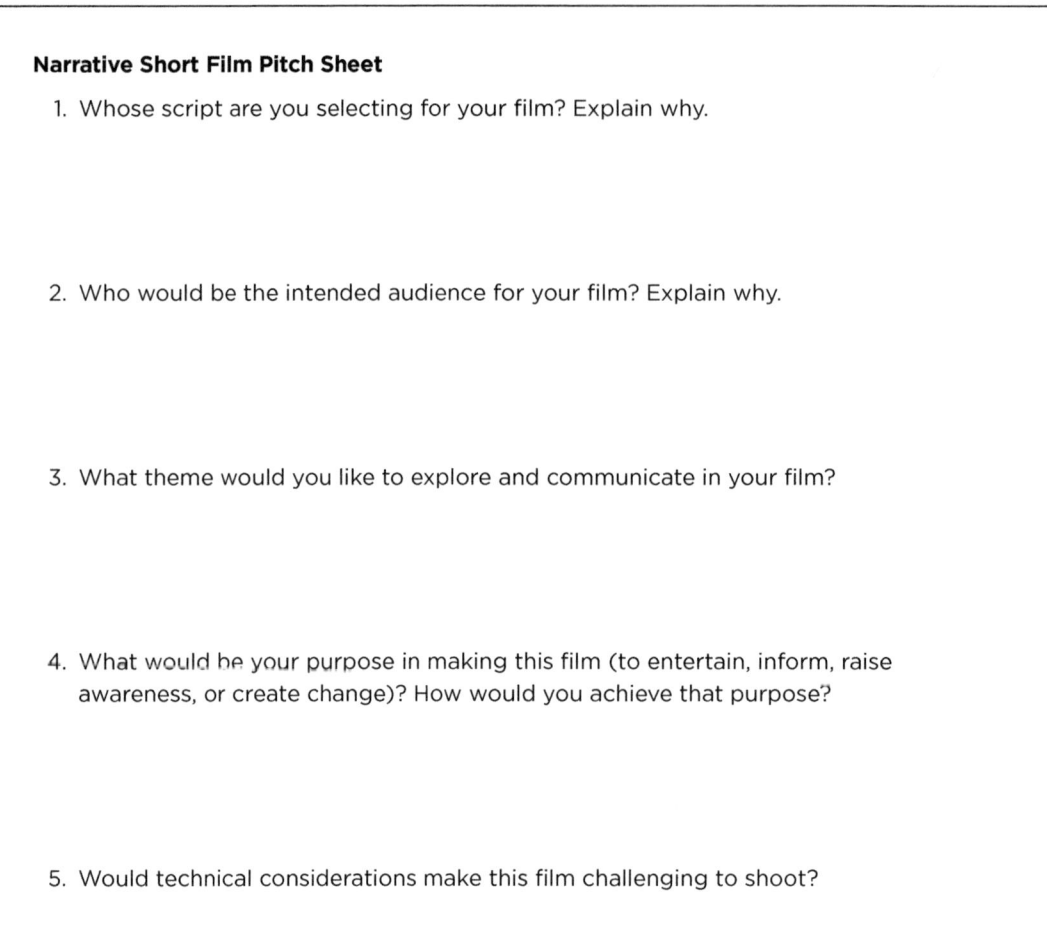

**FIGURE 7.4:** *Narrative short film pitch sheet.*
*Visit **go.SolutionTree.com/technology** for a free reproducible version of this figure.*

During these five-minute pitch sessions, I also like to ask quick, probing questions of the whole team to clarify any confusion I might have about the plot or their ability to execute what's written on the page. Sometimes, crews will come to me with a script that is *phenomenal* but would require a budget or special effects that extend far beyond the awesome resources we keep in our sixth-grade storage closet. It is during these pitch sessions that I get to reel my creatives back in and help them find a practical path toward bringing their films to life.

Afterward, I fill out the "Critical Friend Feedback Form" (page 157 in the appendix), letting them know what I liked about their film pitch, what I still wonder about, and one suggestion I have for the group. Sometimes, I invite guests like our school's librarian or media specialist or local filmmakers to conduct these pitching sessions with me, upping the ante for my presenting students and providing them with further feedback. If I determine that their draft script needs more work, then the students go back and rework their concept; however, if a team has a solid script that they are collectively motivated to film, then their project gets the green light, and they move on to step 4.

### Step 4: Create Storyboards for the Film

With their screenplay in hand, each film crew must now sit down and storyboard their film. A storyboard, as you've seen in previous projects, is a graphic organizer that incorporates illustrations and text to help filmmakers plan and previsualize the shots they need to capture during filming. Each crew takes as many copies of the narrative film storyboards shown in figure 7.5 (page 130) as they'll need to storyboard their script, and they should identify one or two students who were particularly skilled at this step during film school to be their crew's storyboard artists.

As students visualize their films, crews should also begin scouting the locations where they will shoot their scenes. As a reminder, students filming in school must secure permission to shoot in their scouted locations—including specific times and dates—from school administrators and the adult who is most responsible for each space. Prior to filming, they also need to confirm the location is still available and profusely thank whoever is allowing them to film there. When my students film at off-site locations before or after school, they need to secure the proper permissions, as well as provide a detailed travel plan to and from their sets and the parents, caregivers, or other responsible adults who will be supervising and supporting them during their shoot.

## Production

Your students are finally ready to begin filming. They now need access to whatever film equipment you have available. Remember, the only two must-have pieces of equipment each film crew needs are a camera and microphone, both of which are included with your students' laptops or mobile devices, but you can review the guidance in chapter 5 (page 77) for a refresher of your options. However, before a film crew starts filming, each student needs to clearly identify and articulate their assigned production role (also in chapter 5). The most typical roles on a narrative short film crew are director, cinematographer (visuals), sound designer (audio), and grip (equipment). To increase efficiency and add some fun on set, make sure film crews also revisit the list of common filmmaking production cues: *quiet on set, camera rolling, roll sound, action,* and *cut*. Finally, review the following information from chapter 5 with students.

- Principles of cinematography (rule of thirds, depth of field, and twelve shot styles)
- Location, lighting, and sound
- Copyright and fair use

### Step 5: Shoot Primary (A-Roll) and Secondary (B-Roll) Footage

The goal of any film shoot is to capture all the visuals needed to tell a particular story. However, to score a three for visuals on our rubric, student filmmakers should shoot a-roll and b-roll footage using a variety of shot styles, lighting, and visual techniques to create a well-composed film. In addition to telling a great story, these short films need to look great, too. The audience should be able to turn off the sound and still enjoy the beautifully framed shots, and the film's message should resonate through its visuals. Students should check the following three things before pressing record.

1. The background and set are clean and uncluttered.
2. The subject is lit in a lovely way.
3. The camera angle draws the viewer into the conversation.

After that, it's "Quiet on set—lights . . . camera . . . action!"

| Scene Description (What's happening here?): | Location and Characters: | Effects, Props, and Wardrobe: |
| --- | --- | --- |
| | Shot Styles: | |
| Shot # _____: | | Shot # _____: |
| Shot # _____: | | Shot # _____: |
| Shot # _____: | | B-roll footage: |

**FIGURE 7.5:** *Narrative film storyboards.*

Visit **go.SolutionTree.com/technology** *for a free reproducible version of this figure.*

Here are my five tips for keeping things cool, calm, and collected throughout your short film production.

1. Maintain an updated sign-out sheet for your digital equipment (refer to figure 5.14, page 98).
2. As video is shot and captured on phones or memory cards, provide each team with a digital project folder on their computer for storing all their footage and any other images, audio, and so on needed for their video. Create three subfolders—video, audio, and other media—within each project folder so filmmakers can stay organized and save time when they get to postproduction (see "Digital Tools and Technology Tips," page 25 in chapter 1).
3. Students can only shoot at locations they have scouted ahead of time.
4. Students can shoot outside of school hours and manage those logistics themselves. However, if students are filming during school, only one group can shoot outside of the classroom at a time. I post a simple shooting calendar where students can sign up for specific dates, times, and locations in the school.
5. Students must shoot at least one safety shot (additional take) for each critical shot.

### Step 6: Record Additional Audio, Including Narration and Sound Effects

There's a reason why a director's first words before filming are *quiet on set*. No matter how pretty or professional a short film might look, bad audio can ruin the whole thing. Throughout a shoot, the sound designer needs to always have their headphones on, listening to the audio being captured for any noises that might distract or impede the audience from hearing the speech or actions. For best results, students should place a lavalier mic on anyone speaking and connect them to their own laptop, smartphone, or other audio recording device. Finally, if sounds on set can be controlled or eliminated (think air conditioners, fans, and machines that buzz or hum), it's the sound designer's job to do so. However, if noises on set are being caused by forces beyond your students' control (such as wind, traffic, or a passing plane), then the crew will either need to wait or relocate before filming.

The following are four useful tips for recording high-quality audio.

1. Eliminate as much background noise as possible before filming.
2. Record thirty seconds of ambient sound to lay over any gaps or b-roll footage in postproduction.
3. Use external mics whenever possible.
4. Record voiceover narration and sound effects in a small, silent room to avoid echoes and ambient sounds.

### Postproduction

Now that all the visual and auditory elements of your students' films have been collected, it's time to combine them into a well-told story and a short, cohesive film. Just as in production, each film crew member should be assigned a clearly defined postproduction role (refer to chapter 5, page 77, for a refresher on this process). The postproduction roles I always assign my students are the director (continuing in this role from production), editor, sound editor, and assistant editor.

While the three editors have individual responsibilities, the director collaborates throughout post-production with all three to connect their collective vision for their narrative short film.

### Step 7: Edit the Film

Throughout production, each film crew has deposited the video, audio, and other media files they've collected into their digital project folder. Now that production is complete, it is the assistant editor's job to review all media files with the director and catalog everything the crew has collected. First, students create three digital folders titled Act 1, Act 2, and Act 3. Working with the director, the assistant editor labels each media file according to its act and a defining characteristic of the clip and then sorts it into the appropriate folder (such as *Act 1—Ismail introduces himself, Act 3—B-roll walking into a house*). This is also a great opportunity to weed out and delete any video or audio files from production that the crew knows they won't use in the final film. However, if there is even a chance that your students may want to include a clip or piece of audio in their edit, make sure they *don't delete it*. I've seen students cry when they realized they deleted a simple reaction shot or quiet comment that would have tied their whole film together. If this happens, make sure to check for a deleted items folder in the application your students are using. Many editing apps keep deleted content recoverable for a preset number of days.

Once sorted, the assistant editor's final job is to import all media files into whatever video editing software your students will be using. From there, the editor can drag those files onto the timeline and begin crafting the story. Thankfully, after plotting out their short films in preproduction and fleshing out their films during production, the director and editor usually enter this stage with a clear understanding of how these pieces should fit together.

Again, the editor's true work is less in telling the story than it is in *crafting* the story. The editor must painstakingly examine the impact a fraction of a second of video might have on the film's overall flow. Editing can be tedious, meticulous work, so make sure each film crew picks the right student for the job. Per my guidance in chapter 5 (page 77), look for the students who can't stand to color outside the lines, use a ruler to rip a piece of paper, and lean in real close when they're cutting with scissors—these students are your editors.

Congratulations! At this point, your students' film clips have been edited together and the puzzle pieces all fit perfectly. Your editor has added titles, credits, and text to the timeline, and their rough cut has the look of a finished product. However, we enjoy films with our eyes and our ears, so it's now time for the sound editor to add the final audiological flourishes to the film. First, they make sure the captured audio and video footage are high-quality and match the lips as they move on the screen; if there are any issues, they work with the director and editor to determine whether clips need to be replaced or if audio needs to be rerecorded. Next, if additional audio needs to be captured (sound effects, voiceover narration, and so on), the sound editor works with the director to record it and import it for the editor to weave into the film. Finally, the sound editor is responsible for downloading and importing music options for the editor (check out the open-source music options in edit the fifteen-second film, page 100 in chapter 5).

Most students naturally understand when a piece of music is tonally and thematically a nice match for their film. Still, I love facilitating conversations about music by scoring my film crews' works with my own horrible musical selections (think carnival music or a funeral dirge). By playfully discussing the kinds of music that don't serve their film, students can more easily articulate the musical elements that would connect with audiences and elevate their narrative films.

### Step 8: Screen the Rough Cut for the Teacher and at Least Two Critical Friends

For this project, screen each film's rough cut on your computer with two different film crews: (1) the crew that shot the film and (2) another crew to review it. Watch the film together and then discuss it using the short film rubric (figure 7.1, page 123) and "Critical Friend Feedback Form" (page 157 in the appendix). This way, you are providing valuable feedback to the filmmakers whose short you've just enjoyed and also sending your crew of reviewers back to work with greater insights and ideas for revising their own films.

### Step 9: Present the Final Product During the Film Festival

While many teachers assign project deadlines or due dates, I prefer to provide my film crews with a release date by which they need to finish their films to premier at our very own film festival.

This step is not a requirement, and you are welcome to disregard the rest of this paragraph. However, after all the hard work you and your students put into this project, a public exhibition and celebration of their creative achievement is certainly deserved and always a hit. It can be as simple as an afternoon or evening screening of your students' films for friends and families at school. Or, depending on where you are, there may also be film festivals by outside organizations that your students can submit their films to. For example, here in Utah, we have the Tumbleweeds Film Festival (https://tumbleweedskids.org), hosted by the Utah Film Center and Utah Education Network, which features a student film competition, activities, and workshops for children of all ages. Either way, I encourage your students to watch their short films on the big screen in front of a live audience, even if it's just in the school cafeteria or auditorium—it's something they'll never forget.

### Step 10: Publish the Film Online and Complete an After-Project Reflection

Whether you're posting your students' short films on your school's learning management system or an online video-sharing platform, you'll want to discuss how broadly your crews want their work distributed and how they hope to reach their target audience. As I've said, my students publish their video projects on our class's YouTube channel, @9thEvermore, because they want their work accessible to other students just like them—that's who they are creating content for. However, most often, my film crews have chosen to post their short films privately because they want to determine exactly who gets to watch them. This is a team decision that every film crew makes together, and I always look forward to facilitating that conversation.

As always, before your digital content creators move on to their next project, have them reflect on their filmmaking experience by completing an "After-Project Reflection Form" (page 158 in the appendix).

## Conclusion

There are few experiences more fun-filled for students than shooting a film with their friends in school. However, this is still a class project, so let's revisit our objective for this assignment: *I will empower my students' voices by teaching them to share their stories and messages with an online audience of viewers.* This project is all about teaching students how to transform what is traditionally a creative writing assignment into a video production, so if you still want your students to do that but in a format that requires less time and coordination than a five-minute short film, here are a few alternative projects to consider.

- Have your students film their stories using props or student-made characters and sets. This allows filmmakers to bring their stories to life in a controlled environment and without the hassles of shooting live actors on location.
- Have your students shoot their stories as a stop-motion video, using a series of photographs or frames to create the illusion of movement. Filmmakers can achieve this effect with actors or props and easy-to-use apps for their phones or other devices.
- Have your students create a slideshow presentation of their stories with photographs and audio recorded to play over each slide. Students would still need to edit media together to tell a compelling story, learn to record narration, and possibly incorporate music and sound effects into their projects, but without coordinating a film shoot or capturing video in the field.

# CHAPTER 8
# Music Videos

**PROJECT OBJECTIVE**
I will empower my students' voices by teaching them to share their stories and messages through music with an online audience of viewers.

Definition of **Music Video**

**noun**
A videotaped performance of a recorded popular song, usually accompanied by dancing and visual images interpreting the lyrics.

—*Oxford English Dictionary Online*

## CREATORS AT WORK

All my students qualify for free breakfast and lunch, so every morning we watch the news together while my students are eating breakfast. One cold morning, a news story told of a meeting between a U.S. leader and a diverse group of legislators in which the legislators asked why their country should accept immigrants from other countries that he referred to with a mean-spirited expletive.

"Who's he talking about?" my students began to ask.

On cue, the reporter clarified he was referring to countries in Africa, South America, and the Caribbean.

"So, who's he talking about?" I asked.

Juma, who was born of African refugees, said, "I think he's talking about our parents."

Juliana—whose parents had immigrated from Mexico—leaned forward, looked Juma in the eyes, and said, "No, he's talking about *us*!"

A wave of recognition rushed through the room, soon followed by outrage.

Well, my meticulously planned mathematics lesson clearly wasn't happening that morning, so instead, I dipped into my teacher's toolbox and wrote a sentence frame on the board.

*I am angry because _____.*

I gave each student a scratch piece of paper and let them finish the sentence as many times as they wanted. Then, I wrote a second sentence frame on the board.

*The best thing about immigrants is _____.*

135

I said, "It's totally fine to be upset, but if you disagree with what you just heard, you now need to write your rebuttal. Come up with an argument in favor of admitting immigrants like my mom, your parents, and *you* into the United States that will move people when they hear it."

I figured three sentence frames were just right for one day, so I wrote one more.

*The United States brings in people from all over the world because _____.*

That night, as I read through my students' sentences at my kitchen table, I formed the idea of having my students create a music video (to be assessed with the rubric in figure 8.1, page 137) to express their feelings. As I read, one sentence written by Juliana almost made me cry: "The United States brings in people from all over the world because they bring their children, too."

That sentence became our thesis statement.

Scan the QR code to see my students' video, "No More Waiting."

**TEACHERS AND STUDENTS HAVE** been creating music videos for educational purposes since music videos existed. From covers and parodies of popular songs to cheesy raps produced by hilarious educators, music videos are an engaging learning tool for both the creators and their audience. I show music videos in my own classroom to enhance my students' comprehension and retention of key concepts and vocabulary in mathematics, science, social studies, and language arts. The best part about creating music videos, in my opinion, is the sense of community it builds, both in my classroom and across the school. Many of my favorite student- and teacher-produced music videos involve the school's entire faculty and student body, whether behind the scenes in production or in the on-screen singing and dancing. Music videos can also be shared with the wider school community during assemblies and parent events, fostering a sense of belonging and shared accomplishment among students, teachers, and parents alike.

My students make at least one music video as a class every year, each a new contribution to the ever-evolving conversation in the United States.

Scan the QR code to check out all the music videos my students have made over the years, from a Harlem Shake about how to properly punctuate quotes to a song about their experiences as students during the COVID-19 pandemic.

Before students begin their projects, they must first understand the characteristics and components of a well-made music video. Providing model music videos, such as the following, for students to evaluate with the music video rubric (figure 8.1) is a great way to clarify your expectations for students' final products and what success can look like on this project.

|  | 3 | 2 | 1 |
|---|---|---|---|
| **Content** | The video shares an interesting story or message that moves the audience's thoughts or actions. | The video tells a story or communicates a message to the audience. | The video's story or message is unclear. |
| **Narrative Structure** | The video has an excellent hook that engages the audience. There is a clear beginning, middle, and end to the video. | The video has a good hook for the audience. There is some sense of a beginning, middle, and end to the video. | The video lacks an organized structure. |
| **Visuals** | Well-designed shot styles, lighting, and visual techniques are used in the video. The video makes excellent use of both a-roll and b-roll footage. | Good shot styles, lighting, and visual techniques are used in the video. The video makes use of both a-roll and b-roll footage. | The video's look is basic and unengaging to the audience. The video does not use a-roll and b-roll footage in a thoughtful way. |
| **Audio** | The video features high-quality recordings of singing and narrations that are clear and easy to understand. The music and words nicely complement one another. | The video features singing and narrations that the audience can hear and understand. The music and words work OK together. | The video's audio recordings are low quality and distracting. The music and words do not work well together. |
| **Editing** | Deliberate editing decisions move the video forward from beginning to end. Seamless integration of transitions and thoughtful cuts are used in the video. | Some editing decisions help move the video along. Transitions and cuts are used in the video. | Poor editing leaves the video feeling slow or hard to understand. Few or no transitions or cuts are used in the video. |

**FIGURE 8.1:** *Music video rubric.*

*Visit **go.SolutionTree.com/technology** for a free reproducible version of this figure.*

- **John Lewis and Nonviolent Action (www.youtube.com/watch?v=MaQ7tRQ7pBM):** This song, written and performed by a ninth-grade student, was the 2019 Flocabulary's Black History Rap Contest winner. The song focuses on civil rights activist and U.S. Representative John Lewis and his contributions to the fight for civil rights. Flocabulary requires a paid subscription for much of its content, but this video and several others are available to view for free.
- **Too Late to Apologize (www.youtube.com/watch?v=uZfRaWAtBVg):** This parody of the song "Apologize" by OneRepublic provides entertaining insights into the founding fathers' thoughts and motivations as they debated and drafted the Declaration of Independence. This video was clearly professionally made, but it still shows young creators how great lighting and composition can elevate a music video's quality. In fact, my students were so inspired by certain shots in this video that they framed much of their footage in "No More Waiting" after it.
- **The Number Line Dance (www.youtube.com/watch?v=6EWq9EZmIKg):** My friend, teacher, and author, Alex Kajitani—better known to many as The Rappin' Mathematician—created this video about positive and negative numbers with his students way back in 2008. My students always get a kick out of the video quality and vibe of the beat, but they also always understand the relationship between positive and negative numbers and their placement on the number line much better by the end of the song.

I will do something a little different for this digital project. The perspectives and poetry in each of my students' music videos are distinct, but our creative process has remained the same over the years. So, in this chapter, I'm going to take you through that process with a behind-the-scenes look at the making of "No More Waiting" as our model.

## The Project

In this digital project, your creators will produce either one music video as a whole-class project or multiple music videos in smaller film crews with assigned roles. The music video planning page shown in figure 8.2 outlines the steps students follow to successfully complete this digital project.

Stop me if you've heard it already, but there are three stages of video production: (1) preproduction, (2) production, and (3) postproduction. Your student film crews will progress through these project stages at their own pace, so while you'll want to revisit film concepts, production roles, and so on as a class (see chapter 5, page 77), you will also want to allot time during class and outside of school hours for students to work on their music videos, wherever they are in the process.

### *Preproduction*

Preproduction for a music video is heavily focused on writing outstanding lyrics for a chosen song—if the words aren't right, everything else will just feel wrong. As I mentioned, while I have completed this project nearly every year, I have only ever done so with my entire class working on

| **Filmmakers:** | **Music Video Title and Topic:** |
|---|---|
| **Preproduction** | |
| Step 1: Select and outline the song. | |
| Step 2: Brainstorm individual lines for the song. | |
| Step 3: Organize lines into verses. | |
| Step 4: Complete a final draft of the song. | |
| **Production** | |
| Step 5: Record audio of singing and spoken lines. | |
| Step 6: Edit the recorded audio together with the music. | |
| Step 7: Shoot primary (a-roll) and secondary (b-roll) footage. | |
| **Postproduction** | |
| Step 8: Edit the music video: song and video, still images, transitions, effects, and credits. | |
| Step 9: Screen the rough cut for the teacher and at least two critical friends. Continue editing as needed. | |
| Step 10: Publish the music video online and complete an After-Project Reflection. | |

**FIGURE 8.2:** *Music video planning.*

*Visit **go.SolutionTree.com/technology** for a free reproducible version of this figure.*

one music video together. However, all steps from preproduction through postproduction can be easily adapted to support smaller groups organized into film crews like those in chapters 6 and 7.

### Step 1: Select and Outline the Song

Choosing the right song to cover can take minutes or weeks. You might come into this project with a song in mind, or your students will come up with the perfect tune in class. Either way, here are five things to think about as you and your students select your songs.

1. **Choice:** Creators will invest more time and energy in a song they had some say in selecting.
2. **Age appropriateness:** Songs must be suitable for your students' age group and align with any guidelines or restrictions set by the school or parents.
3. **Relevance and connection:** Select a song that holds some meaning for your students or resonates with the project's theme.
4. **Song structure and length:** Songs need a clear structure (verse, chorus, and bridge) and should be reasonable in length. Basically, don't cover Queen's "Bohemian Rhapsody" unless you're these calculus students—https://rb.gy/15x7k2 (Gospel & Kirk, 2009).
5. **Performance opportunities:** Consider if the chosen song offers opportunities for creative interpretation or performance elements that can enhance the project, like dance choreography, costume design, or other visual elements.

Copyright is also a key consideration when selecting songs for any digital project. You need to be able to distinguish between copyright infringement versus fair use, as described in the activity "copyright infringement or fair use?" (page 20). Remember, as explained in that activity, the legal doctrine of fair use allows teachers and students to use copyrighted materials in educational settings depending on certain conditions, including whether the use is commercial or for nonprofit educational purposes. My students have never run into any issues with their music videos because their covers are created strictly for educational purposes, are not released commercially, and we always provide proper attribution to the original song titles and artists.

When making song selections, it's important to draw connections between the song's context, mood, and style and the message students want to deliver. Following our class discussion about immigration, someone suggested we cover the song "Praying" by Kesha, and our search for the perfect song was over. The melody of Kesha's song matched my students' emotions, and her lyrics connected thematically with their responses to the sentence frames. However, the music in her studio version swells so dramatically toward the end that it would have been impossible to hear my students' voices over the song, so we hopped online and found a softer instrumental version that communicated the same emotions but left more room for my students' voices to shine.

Once you've chosen your song, outline its lyrical structure to see the number of stanzas and individual lines your students will need to write. As your writers brainstorm and draft their lyrics, this outline will ensure their words fit within the song's blueprint. For example, figure 8.3 shows the lyrical outline for my students' cover of "Praying."

### Step 2: Brainstorm Individual Lines for the Song

I wrote two sentence frames on the board every day for a week after students watched the instigating news story to inspire their lyrics. By the time everyone's responses were collected, my students had over four hundred lines to choose from. Sorting through all these individual lines took time, and it would have been easier just to have one or two students write the whole song for us; still, I run these brainstorming sessions because it's the best way I've found to ensure every student has lines that make it into the song.

After we brainstorm, I have several students type each line into a word processor document, along with the writer's name. They then review the document together, deleting any lines that are identical or redundant and saving a copy of the original just in case they accidentally delete any treasures. Consider doing the following to help students brainstorm lyrics.

1. Write the topic or theme of your song on the board.
2. Have your students shout out words, phrases, or lines that connect to your topic or theme.
3. Play your chosen song and decide on a solid first line together. Then, continue playing the song and give students five to ten minutes to independently write lines that could build on the topic or theme from there.
4. After brainstorming their lines, students share what they've written with their peers.
5. Depending on how many lines you want to work with, have each student select their top three to five lines to turn in for consideration as lyrics for the class's song.

If you want to make music videos as a small-group project rather than as a whole class, then adapt this same activity by allowing each group to develop a solid first line for their chosen song, topic, or theme and then brainstorm from there.

| | | |
|---|---|---|
| **Verse 1**<br>(four lines,<br>sixteen beats) | 1.<br>2.<br>3.<br>4. | |
| **Verse 2**<br>(four lines,<br>sixteen beats) | 5.<br>6.<br>7.<br>8. | |
| **Verse 3**<br>(four lines,<br>sixteen beats) | 9.<br>10.<br>11.<br>12. | |
| **Chorus**<br>(twelve lines,<br>forty-eight beats) | 13.<br>14.<br>15.<br>16.<br>17.<br>18.<br>19.<br>20.<br>21.<br>22.<br>23.<br>24. | |
| **Verse 4**<br>(four lines,<br>sixteen beats) | 25.<br>26.<br>27.<br>28. | |
| **Verse 5**<br>(four lines,<br>sixteen beats) | 29.<br>30.<br>31.<br>32. | |

***FIGURE 8.3:*** *Lyrical outline.*

| | | |
|---|---|---|
| **Verse 6**<br>(four lines,<br>sixteen beats) | 33. | |
| | 34. | |
| | 35. | |
| | 36. | |
| **Verse 7**<br>(six lines,<br>twenty-four beats) | 37. | |
| | 38. | |
| | 39. | |
| | 40. | |
| | 41. | |
| | 42. . | |
| **CHORUS** | | |
| **Verse 8**<br>(four lines,<br>sixteen beats) | 43. | |
| | 44. | |
| | 45. | |
| | 46. | |
| **Verse 9**<br>(four lines,<br>sixteen beats) | 47. | |
| | 48. | |
| | 49. | |
| | 50. | |
| **CHORUS** | | |

### *Step 3: Organize Lines Into Verses*

When I passed out packets with all my students' brainstormed lines, students read each other's words, and their heads started nodding; they made eye contact, pointed at the paper with approval, and quickly began shouting their approval from across the room. Just like that, one unfortunate news story had transformed my class into a writers' room.

When they finished reading, we discussed the themes surfacing in their song, such as the hardships refugees faced in their home countries and traits shared by the children of immigrants. These themes stemmed largely from the sentence frames that prompted each response, and yet there were brilliant lines written on different days by different writers that connected so beautifully it felt like fate.

For instance, in response to the question, What's the best thing about immigrants from difficult places? one student wrote, "Those people are tough and hard, and yet still full of love." Another student wrote, "Their dreams came true." Then, completing a completely different sentence stem—We should celebrate immigrants from difficult places because . . .—a third student wrote, "Because they were able to rise above." Jasmine, a shy student who loved words and hated attention, quietly put those three lines together on her paper.

*Those people are tough and hard, and yet still full of love*
*Because they were able to rise above*
*And their dreams came true*

With the packet of lines in one hand and lined paper in the other, my writers worked in small groups to combine those lines into stanzas like puzzle pieces, grouping lines that shared a similar idea or message into verses with four lines and sixteen beats each. It reminded me of a creative writing assignment I had in high school, where we took random lines cut out of magazines and newspapers and glued them into poems on blank sheets of paper. The difference, of course, was that each line my students placed before or after another was written by a friend about a loved one they feared was under attack. So, when each group shared their draft verses, the level of engagement and grace my kids showed one another gave me goosebumps.

The next day, I made copies of the various verses and taped them around the room, grouping similar stanzas together so students could consider them side by side. Then, I gave each student three sticky notes to place on their favorite verses as votes; the only rule was that they couldn't put a sticky note on any of their group's work. By the end of the activity, we had a ranked list of outstanding verses to try plugging into our song. Here are some ways I've found success with helping students combine lyrics into verses.

1. Start with the lines students brainstormed in step 2. Divide your class into small groups, assigning each group a single verse to compose with a specific idea that needs to be communicated in your song.
2. Have students find lines from the list that fit that idea and sort them into verses. If none of the lines fit quite right, students can take turns writing lines or collaboratively composing them together.
3. Once a verse is complete, have students revise to ensure the lines cohesively work together and fit within the verse's sixteen beats.
4. Have a spokesperson from each group read aloud their verses to the class.

If each small group is making their own music video, then adapt this activity to provide enough time for them to compose all the verses and chorus for their song.

### Step 4: Complete a Final Draft of the Song

Once my class had a strong collection of verses, each with four lines and sixteen beats, I met with one small group of writers after another to complete a final draft of the song. Working with my students was incredible as they revised their lyrics down to the word level, syllable by syllable, tweaking each line to fit comfortably within the four-count structure. When they finished tying up their lyrical loose ends—adding a couple of lines to verse seven and smoothing out a few syllabic bumps in their final draft (figure 8.4, page 144)—my writers came away with a song whose words were just as lovely without the music.

| | |
|---|---|
| **Verse 1**<br>(four lines,<br>sixteen beats) | 1. This one's for all the kids out there<br>2. Whose ancestors were immigrants, whose parents are immigrants<br>3. Whose friends are immigrants, who are immigrants<br>4. Just like us |
| **Verse 2**<br>(four lines,<br>sixteen beats) | 5. You know the best part about immigrants, especially immigrants<br>6. From difficult places, places where life was rough<br>7. Countries and cities where there wasn't enough<br>8. Where people look back and say, "Life's not easy there." |
| **Verse 3**<br>(four lines,<br>sixteen beats) | 9. You know the best thing about immigrants from places like that?<br>10. The thing they bring that makes our country so much better?<br>11. So much better? It's their children, their kids<br>12. The children of immigrants, us! Especially now |
| **Chorus**<br>(twelve lines,<br>forty-eight beats) | 13. 'Cause we fought the flames and we've all been through hell<br>14. We had to learn how to fight for ourselves<br>15. Now we've found the beauty in the truth we have to tell<br>16. So, we'll just say this as we wish you farewell<br>17. I know you're out there praying<br>18. Praying<br>19. I know your soul is changing<br>20. Changing<br>21. But we'll only find our peace<br>22. In fighting for our dreams<br>23. No more<br>24. Waiting |
| **Verse 4**<br>(four lines,<br>sixteen beats) | 25. The reason our country brings in people from all over the world<br>26. And not just the places that are doing really well<br>27. Is because people who suffered, who survived their struggle<br>28. People who lost everything, over and over |
| **Verse 5**<br>(four lines,<br>sixteen beats) | 29. And still, somehow, made it all the way here<br>30. Those people are tough and hard, and yet still full of love<br>31. Because they were able to rise above, and their dreams came true<br>32. No more waiting |
| **Verse 6**<br>(four lines,<br>sixteen beats) | 33. Those people are amazing! But you better look out<br>34. Because their kids, we're even more intimidating<br>35. We've grown up humble and respecting our elders<br>36. They never let us forget that we have it better than they ever did |

| **Verse 7**<br>(six lines,<br>twenty-four beats) | 37. They don't let us take it for granted |
| --- | --- |
| | 38. We're gritty and grateful, we're old world and new |
| | 39. We have to work twice as hard to get half as much |
| | 40. Should we have to? Doesn't matter, we have to, so let's go! |
| | 41. It's all good, we'll work five times as hard, ten times |
| | 42. Whatever it takes, that's what's up! |
| **CHORUS** | |
| **Verse 8**<br>(four lines,<br>sixteen beats) | 43. This isn't just a fight, this is a trial |
| | 44. Our families are being judged; people question what we're worth |
| | 45. As kids, we represent the best we have to offer |
| | 46. So, we can't wait around, we have to lead by example! |
| **Verse 9**<br>(four lines,<br>sixteen beats) | 47. Work hard, get good grades, help others in need |
| | 48. Volunteer, start a career, and uplift your family. We can do this! |
| | 49. And when the fools come at us daily |
| | 50. We'll succeed and persevere, and it will drive them crazy |
| **CHORUS** | |

**FIGURE 8.4:** *Final draft of lyrics.*

Consider doing the following to complete a final draft of a song with your students.

1. Assemble a small team of student editors to situate and revise your best verses within your song's outline.
2. Empower them to amend, delete, and write lines as needed.
3. Have one student read the lyrics aloud to the class, soliciting feedback on any final revisions they feel should be made.

If students are creating their own music videos in small groups, they each can complete this step together as a team.

## *Production*

Creating a music video requires both audio- and video-production skills. Students sing and speak into microphones, record audio over a music track, edit it together, and then film themselves lip-syncing to their song before finally combining all the sights and sounds in their finished product.

That's a lot.

To keep it simple, I assemble what I like to call my super crew—the top director, cinematographer, sound mixer, and editor in each class—and they do 90 percent of the work for the rest of us. Once that super crew has a final draft of the lyrics in hand, they develop a visual concept for the music video using the audio- and video-editing organizer shown in figure 8.5 (page 146). They determine together shoot locations, production design elements, shot styles, and lighting design. If your students are making music videos in small groups, each group should be organized as its own super crew.

| A-Roll Footage: Shots you need in your music video. | B-Roll Footage: Additional footage |
|---|---|
| **Shoot Locations:** **Production Design:** **Shot Styles:** **Lighting Design:** | 1. <br> 2. <br> 3. <br> 4. <br> 5. |

| Song Line | Performer | Performance and Production Notes |
|---|---|---|
|  |  |  |
|  |  |  |
|  |  |  |
|  |  |  |
|  |  |  |

**FIGURE 8.5:** *Audio- and video-editing organizer.*

*Visit **go.SolutionTree.com/technology** for a free reproducible version of this figure.*

Before filming, the super crew must complete all the typical preproduction steps for a film shoot, including the following.

1. Scouting locations and securing permissions to film
2. Collecting all props, costumes, and film equipment
3. Storyboarding as needed
4. Rehearsing with performers
5. Preparing sets with the design elements that create visually appealing shots

During my first two years of teaching, I did most of the production work for our music videos myself (that's why they're not as good). Those videos were busy, piecing together handheld shots in multiple locations and all different angles. In my third year of teaching, I turned the production reins over to my first super crew, and they came up with the idea of putting the camera on a tripod and using one medium shot, seating each performer in the middle of the room with a single lamp to light them. They also placed classmates over the shoulder of each subject—standing tall in solidarity behind them—using depth of field to blur these powerful figures. The simplicity of their production design has provided the creative framework for every music video we've made since then.

Scan the QR code to watch my students affirm the value and dignity of the United States' immigrant communities.

### Step 5: Record Audio of Singing and Spoken Lines

My super crew filled in their organizer (figure 8.5) with every line of "No More Waiting," the performer who would read each line, and any notes they felt were needed to deliver the line in just the right way. The director and sound mixer pulled students one at a time into the quiet recording space we set up in our roomy sixth-grade storage closet with just my MacBook, GarageBand, and a microphone (see chapter 4, page 61, for tips on recording quality audio). They recorded at least three solid takes of each line and then saved all their audio files in the digital project folder for this music video (see "Digital Tools and Technology Tips," page 25 in chapter 1).

Before recording, I had asked my class if anyone was willing to sing the song's chorus. Sadly, no one raised their hand. Later that day, I was getting ready to bother a couple of students who I knew could carry a tune when Viliamu, a young football player with a somewhat raspy voice, came to my desk and whispered, "I can sing." No lie, I was incredibly skeptical. Still, we went into the hall, and Viliamu sang the chorus for me. Having seen the video yourself (if you accessed the "No More Waiting" QR code at the start of this chapter), you know that boy's voice is magical—I just had no idea he'd been hiding it all that time. I immediately sent him into the recording room with our sound mixer, and he nailed the chorus in the first two takes.

This is just one example of how, in my experience, every classroom has at least one student who sings like an angel. However, sometimes they need a little coaching to hit all the right notes. I am absolutely *not* a singing coach, but I have learned a few tips over the years to help students deliver a solid vocal performance, including the following.

- **Vocal warm-ups:** Before exercising any muscles in the body, you must warm them up to prevent strains or injuries. There are plenty of fun ways to loosen up your vocal cords: humming like a bumblebee, pretending to be a car starting up, or singing the alphabet song as fast as you can.
- **Breathing techniques:** Singers need to take deep breaths from their diaphragm instead of shallow breaths from their chest. To make it playful, they can pretend to blow bubbles or blow feathers to practice this technique.
- **Sing karaoke in class:** Karaoke isn't for everybody, but it's always been an awesome brain break in my class and a low-stakes practice opportunity for my up-and-coming singers.
- **Embrace your voice:** Everyone has a unique voice, and it's crucial for young singers to embrace theirs rather than imitating a famous artist they admire. There's no harm in

introducing them to various singers to inspire their own style, but authenticity is what we enjoy most when students step up to the mic.

### Step 6: Edit the Recorded Audio Together With the Music

Once everyone finished recording their lines, the director and sound mixer went through and listened to all the audio files recorded in GarageBand. Again, there were at least three recordings for each line, so this step took a couple of days of working before and after school, and my students *loved* it. Starting with the first line, they played each of the three performances over the music, then kept the one they thought fit best and deleted the rest.

Here are a few tips to help this step run smoothly.

- Keep a backup file with all the original recordings, just in case.
- When there is a disagreement between the director and sound mixer on which performance to keep, bring in the editor and cinematographer to help decide. If the vote is still split, you become the deciding vote.
- Keep the volume on the music track turned down enough to best hear the students' lines clearly.
- When you finish and export the audio file, use the highest quality export option you have available—preferably WAV or AIFF, but if you must compress your audio file because it's too large, use AAC instead of MP3.

### Step 7: Shoot Primary (A-Roll) and Secondary (B-Roll) Footage

Finally, we recorded our music video. The super crew positioned a forty-dollar ring light on a stand at the front of our classroom, about eight feet from the wall. They set my DSLR camera on a tripod pointed through the center of the ring light and turned off the other lights in the room. As I taught mathematics behind them, my crew filmed each student one at a time lip-syncing along to their prerecorded parts with their back to my SMART Board, the song playing loud enough for the camera's microphone to capture it clearly (a key piece for postproduction). Sure, at first, it was distracting for some of the students I was teaching, but after a while, everyone lost interest in what was happening up front until it was their turn to perform. In one day, we shot all our a-roll footage, and the outtakes from that shoot became our b-roll footage. A couple of students struggled to mouth their lines correctly while staring into the camera, but otherwise, everything went smoothly, and even my shyest students delivered strong performances.

The degree of difficulty involved in your shoot will depend on the complexity of your students' vision for their music video. These five tips will help you maintain calm and focus throughout production, especially if your students are filming their own music videos in small groups.

1. Maintain an updated sign-out sheet for your digital equipment (refer to figure 5.14, page 98).
2. As video is shot and captured on phones or memory cards, provide each team with a digital project folder on their computer for storing all their footage and any other images, audio, and so on needed for their video. Create three subfolders—video, audio, and other media—within each project folder so filmmakers can stay organized and save time when they get to postproduction (see "Digital Tools and Technology Tips," page 25 in chapter 1).

3. Students can only shoot at locations they have scouted ahead of time.
4. Students can shoot outside of school hours and manage those logistics themselves. However, if students are filming during school, only one group can shoot outside of the classroom at a time. I post a simple shooting calendar where students can sign up for specific dates, times, and locations in the school.
5. Students need to shoot at least one safety shot (additional take) for each critical shot.

## Postproduction

Postproduction on a music video is straightforward, because your song provides the road map—you know which clips go where because the performances you see on screen must align with the song's words. From this point on, the students' workflows should be the same regardless of whether it's a whole-class project or a series of small-group projects.

### Step 8: Edit the Music Video

The editor's first job is to go through all the video files collected during the shoot with the director. Their goal is to quickly sweep the files for any failed takes that can immediately be deleted. Next, they import the remaining files into the film editing software, along with their high-quality audio recording of the song.

The trickiest step in editing a music video is getting the words to look like they're coming from the performer's lips. That's why it's so helpful to play the song at a good volume while shooting—to sync the audio and visual elements together, the audio tracks from the camera and the computer need to line up perfectly.

Working together, the director and editor select all the individual takes for each line they think best align with the song's audio track, shaving fractions of a second off either end of each clip to make them fit just right. After that, they apply whatever filters and effects they need to achieve the final look of the music video. On "No More Waiting," this meant selecting a filter to apply to every clip, brightening shots that were a touch too dark, saturating the entire video, and even adding a few tasteful lens flares to the performances during the chorus. In only a couple of days, they had a rough cut ready to view.

### Step 9: Screen the Rough Cut for the Teacher and at Least Two Critical Friends

The audience for this project's rough cut should be the cinematographer, the sound mixer, and you. Screen the rough cut together, using the "Critical Friend Feedback Form" (page 157 in the appendix) as a guide for your discussion. For "No More Waiting," we watched the music video together while the other students were out at recess. As we discussed the video, we decided there were a few minor tweaks in the timing that needed to be worked out, but otherwise it was perfect. And yet, something didn't feel quite right about it.

When the students came back from recess, we decided to show it to the whole class. Again, everyone thought it was amazing, though something about the video felt wrong to me. It wasn't until much later that it finally hit me: Their music video was *too* good. The words, the singing, the production value—all of it was too perfect, too polished. I remembered how emotional my students had been on that first day, when all they could do was finish sentence stems on scratch paper. That raw emotion wasn't there on the screen, and I missed it.

That evening, I wandered the halls of Meadowlark Elementary, capturing b-roll footage of posters and student artwork on the walls. I recorded quick clips in my classroom of the chair that wasn't pushed in at the end of the day, and the pens and colored pencils students had used hours earlier to create beautiful things.

The next morning, I interviewed a handful of students, asking them how they were feeling about immigration now that their project was over, what they were afraid of, and the best part about being a part of their culture?

I gave the footage and audio to my director and editor and asked them to create an introduction to the music video, no more than forty-five seconds, that would let everyone know how the students in our class were honestly feeling. They had a rough cut ready by the next day. It was better than I could have hoped for, and in between that night and the next morning, I posted their video online.

### Step 10: Publish the Music Video Online and Complete an After-Project Reflection

If this is the first video your students have produced, you will want to revisit the options for publishing their project online in chapter 5 (page 77). Essentially, the choice comes down to making it available only to your students and their families or posting their work where everyone can see. This is their project, so I always let them decide; however, if they have created work that contributes to an ongoing conversation in the public discourse, I always encourage my students to make their voices heard and let others benefit from their brilliance.

As for the filmmakers featured in this chapter, we published their video on our YouTube channel twelve days after the students first saw the news story. On the same morning that I posted their music video on YouTube, Jacqueline Woodson (2014), author of *Brown Girl Dreaming*, came to visit our class. We had read her book in anticipation of her visit; alone in our classroom, she spent over an hour reading us her poems and telling us stories from her childhood that had inspired her work. Then, before she left, a student asked if she'd like to see the music video they had just made. Soon after, she shared the video on her social media account and wrote:

> I spent the morning with these beautiful young Ambassadors in their classroom in Salt Lake City, Utah. Their teacher is everything. This video is even more. I LOVE my job!! #Dreamers. (Woodson, 2018)

I'll be honest, I didn't make my students complete an "After-Project Reflection Form" (page 158 in the appendix) for this one—if they ever stopped talking about *that* music video they made together, I might have considered it.

## Conclusion

Let's revisit this project's objective: *I will empower my students' voices by teaching them to share their stories and messages through music with an online audience of viewers.* Those stories and messages can be hilarious, heartwarming, and anything else your students want them to be. If you want your students to create videos that meaningfully combine music with words but want to start with something simpler than the project I've described, here are a few other ideas for your content creators to consider.

- **Cover song:** Record yourself covering a song without changing any of the lyrics. Choose a song whose words resonate with you and say the things you want to say. You can also put your own spin on the song by creating a new musical arrangement for your cover.
- **Spoken word:** Write poetic lines inspired by a song and record yourself reading your words over the song's instrumental track as a spoken-word performance.
- **Slideshow:** Create a slideshow presentation with photographs and video clips to play over a song you love, providing a visual display to accompany the words and music.

# EPILOGUE

**THROUGHOUT THIS BOOK,** you've gained insights into innovative practices that replace old assignments with digital projects, providing new platforms for your students' self-expression, creativity, and personal development, as well as mastery of grade-level standards. Along the way, you have also explored the transformative potential of reframing your students as content creators who are empowered by the work completed in your classroom.

Now, if you haven't already, you get to pick the first digital project you want to implement with your students. As you decide, I want to reiterate that, above all else, one of the key goals of this work should be to empower and amplify students' individual and collective voices. By encouraging our students to explore their passions through digital media, we are showing them their thoughts, ideas, and perspectives are not only valuable, but necessary. I'm not exaggerating when I say we *need* our students to use technology to create content that can help us better understand our youth, learn from their lived experiences, and heal our world. Young people recognize that we live in a world where far too many voices go unheard, where certain perspectives are marginalized, and where inequities persist. By providing underrepresented students with digital outlets for creative expression, you are taking a step toward greater equality, equity, and justice in our schools. This is not just about individual empowerment—it's about making a collective difference. These projects are not just assignments, they are vehicles for personal and societal change.

There is no reason students from high school down to elementary students like mine should be waiting until they're older to exercise their voices in service to causes *they* believe in. While others wait until after they graduate from high school or college to make a difference, my students will be able to look back on over a decade of impact by the time they leave university. Our students are the most effective champions we have for solving our toughest issues, and it's up to us, their teachers, to get them in the game.

From the bottom of my heart, thank you for embracing and elevating our students' voices. And please, reach out and let me know how I can find and amplify your students' work—I can't wait to enjoy all the content they will create!

# APPENDIX

**THE FOLLOWING DOCUMENTS** support the projects detailed throughout this book. Visit **go.SolutionTree.com/technology** to download reproducible versions of these tools.

# Five Fascinating Facts Form

Now that you have chosen a topic, it is time to do your research and find information to present to your audience. You may use books and other texts, along with online research tools, to find the five most fascinating facts related to your topic. Don't forget to cite your sources.

| Fact | Source |
| --- | --- |
| 1. | |
| 2. | |
| 3. | |
| 4. | |
| 5. | |

# Critical Friend Feedback Form

A critical friend is a classmate who is committed to helping you improve as a content creator. A critical friend is encouraging and supportive, and they can be trusted to provide constructive, honest feedback on specific ways you can improve your work.

| Critical Friend | Content Creator | Project Title |
|---|---|---|
|  |  |  |

I Like . . .

I Wonder . . .

I Suggest . . .

# After-Project Reflection

| Content Creator | Project Title | Date |
|---|---|---|
|  |  |  |

**I Like:** What were things you liked or appreciated about your project and the creative process? What did you do well? What choices did you make that elevated your work?

**I Wonder:** What might you have done differently during the creative process, and how would that have affected your project's outcome?

**Next Steps:** Going forward as a content creator, what will you do to improve your creative process and the work you produce?

**The Digital Projects Playbook** © 2025 Solution Tree Press • SolutionTree.com
Visit **go.SolutionTree.com/technology** to download this free reproducible.

# REFERENCES AND RESOURCES

Alsamadani, H. A. (2018). The effectiveness of using online blogging for students' individual and group writing. *International Education Studies, 11*(1), 44–51.

Blasco, P. G., Moreto, G., Blasco, M. G., Levites, M. R., & Janaudis, M. A. (2015). Education through movies: Improving teaching skills and fostering reflection among students and teachers. *Journal for Learning through the Arts, 11*(1).

Blog. (n.d.). In *Merriam-Webster's online dictionary*. Accessed at www.merriam-webster.com/dictionary/blog on May 21, 2024.

Bouchey, B., Castek, J., & Thygeson, J. (2021). Multimodal learning. In J. Ryoo & K. Winkelmann (Eds.), *Innovative Learning Environments in STEM Higher Education* (pp. 35–54). Cham, Switzerland: Springer Nature Switzerland AG.

Cain, J., Cain, S., & Daigle, B. (2021). Constructivist podcasting strategies in the 8th grade social studies classroom: "StudyCasts" support motivation and learning outcomes. *The Social Studies, 112*(6), 310–321.

Campillo-Ferrer, J. M., Miralles-Martinez, P., & Sanchez-Ibanez, R. (2021). The effectiveness of using edublogs as an instructional and motivating tool in the context of higher education. *Humanities and Social Sciences Communications, 8*(175).

Charlop-Christy, M. H., Le, L., & Freeman, K. A. (2001). A comparison of video modeling with in vivo modeling for teaching children with autism. *Journal of Autism and Developmental Disorders, 30*(6), 537–552.

Clark, D. (2018). *How much should you charge for a speech?* Accessed at https://hbsp.harvard.edu/product/H04B45-PDF-ENG on February 2, 2024.

Dabrowski, J., & Marshall, T. R. (2018). *Motivation and engagement in student assignments: The role of choice and relevancy*. Washington, DC: The Education Trust. Accessed at https://files.eric.ed.gov/fulltext/ED593328.pdf on February 2, 2024.

Dewey, J. (1916). *Democracy and education*. New York: Columbia University Press.

Dickson, S. (2023, September). *Utah's personalized, competency based learning framework*. Salt Lake City, UT: Utah State Board of Education. Accessed at https://schools.utah.gov/curr/pcbl/_pcbl_/UtahPCBLFramework.pdf on February 2, 2024.

Documentary. (n.d.). In *Oxford English Dictionary's online dictionary*. Accessed at www.oed.com/dictionary/documentary_adj?tab=factsheet#6354311 on May 21, 2024.

Dversnes, G., & Blikstad-Balas, M. (2023) The potential of podcasts for exploratory talk in high school. *Computers in the Schools, 40*(3), 282–302.

Field, S. (1984). *The screenwriter's workbook*. New York: Dell Publishing.

Film. (n.d.). In *Oxford English Dictionary's online dictionary*. Accessed at www.oed.com/search/dictionary/?scope=Entries&q=film on May 20, 2024.

Freire, P. (2017). *Pedagogy of the oppressed*. London: Penguin Classics.

Gospel, M., & Kirk, P. (2009, May 22). *Calculus Rhapsody*. [Video file]. Accessed at www.youtube.com/watch?v=uqwC41RDPyg on May 20, 2024.

Halic, O., Lee, D., Paulus, T., & Spence, M. (2010). To blog or not to blog: Student perceptions of blog effectiveness for learning in a college-level course. *The Internet and Higher Education, 13*(4), 206–213.

Hickman, C., Marks, E., Pihkala, P., Clayton, S., Lewandowski, R. E., Mayall, E. E., et al. (2021). Climate anxiety in children and young people and their beliefs about government responses to climate change: A global survey. *The Lancet, 5*(12), 863–873.

Hitchcock, L. I., Sage, T., Lynch, M., & Sage, M. (2021). Podcasting as a pedagogical tool for experiential learning in social work education. *Journal of Teaching in Social Work, 41*(2), 172–191.

Hough, L. (2022, January 6). *Project-based learning is great, but students still need to learn something.* Accessed at https://www.gse.harvard.edu/ideas/usable-knowledge/22/01/project-based-learning-great-students-still-need-learn-something on February 2, 2024.

Huebner, T. A., & Burstein, R. (2023, June). *Strategies for encouraging technology-enabled instructional practices in K–12 education: A thought piece drawing on research and practice.* San Francisco: WestEd. Accessed at https://www.wested.org/wp-content/uploads/2023/06/Tech-Enabled-Instruction-Thought-Piece_FINAL_ADA.pdf on February 2, 2024.

Jones, L. (2020, January 22). *"It's good to be alive": The Studio Ghibli films are coming to Netflix at just the right time.* Accessed at www.independent.co.uk/arts-entertainment/films/features/studio-ghibli-netflix-movies-my-neighbour-totoro-spirited-away-princess-mononoke-miyazaki-a9297181.html on May 20, 2024.

Kabadayi, L. (2012). The role of short film in education. *Procedia–Social and Behavioral Sciences, 47,* 316–320.

Khan, S. (2015, November). *Let's teach for mastery—not test scores* [Video file]. TED Conferences. Accessed at www.ted.com/talks/sal_khan_let_s_teach_for_mastery_not_test_scores?language=en on May 20, 2024.

Kramer, I. M., & Kusurkar, R. A. (2017). Science-writing in the blogosphere as a tool to promote autonomous motivation in education. *The Internet and Higher Education, 35,* 48–62.

Kuo, Y.-C., Belland, B. R., & Kuo, Y.-T. (2017). Learning through blogging: Students' perspectives in collaborative blog-enhanced learning communities. *Educational Technology and Society, 20*(2), 37–50.

Lagola, K. (2021, March 22). *A teacher's guide to copyright and fair use.* Accessed at www.edutopia.org/article/teachers-guide-copyright-and-fair-use on February 2, 2024.

LePage, P., & Courey, S. (2011). Filmmaking: A video-based intervention for developing social skills in children with autism spectrum disorder. *Interdisciplinary Journal of Teaching and Learning, 1*(2), 88–103.

Levine, E., & Patrick, S. (2019) *What is competency-based learning? An updated definition.* Vienna, VA: CompetencyWorks. Accessed at https://files.eric.ed.gov/fulltext/ED604019.pdf on January 2, 2024.

Liao, M.-K., Lewis, G., & Winiski, M. (2020). Do students learn better with Pecha Kucha, an alternative presentation platform? *Journal of Microbiology and Biology Education, 21*(3).

Mallory, E., Montgomery, S., Ringo, S., & Wray, R. (2018). Learning in focus: The curriculum guide to the Utah Film Center's teacher professional development filmmaking in the classroom. *Utah Film Center,* 15 Edition.

Manfre, J. (2021, July 14) *How a simple presentation framework helps students learn.* Accessed at www.edutopia.org/article/how-simple-presentation-framework-helps-students-learn on February 2, 2024.

McCarron, G., & Yamanaka, A. (2022). The power of the microphone: Podcasting as an effective instructional tool for leadership in education. *Journal of Leadership Education, 21*(14).

McGough, R. (2005). *Collected Poems.* London: Penguin UK.

McLuhan, M. (1964). *Understanding media: The extensions of man.* New York: McGraw-Hill.

Meager, N. (2017). Children make observational films—Exploring a participatory visual method for art education. *International Journal of Education through Art. 13*(1), 7–22.

Montebello, M., Cope, B., Kalantzis, M., Haniya, S., Amina, T., Tzirides, A. O., et al. (2019). Multimodal mastery learning. *International Journal of Learning and Teaching, 5*(1), 19–23.

Moody, R. (2016). *Student presentations: Why they're vital and how to build them into your SoW.* Accessed at https://educationblog.oup.com/secondary/psychology/student-presentations-why-theyre-vital-and-how-to-build-them-into-your-sow on February 2, 2024.

Music video. (n.d.). In *Oxford English Dictionary's online dictionary*. Accessed at https://www.oed.com/dictionary/music-video_n?tab=factsheet#35561616100 on May 21, 2024.

National Association for Media Literacy Education. (2024). *Media literacy defined*. Accessed at https://namle.org/resources/media-literacy-defined on May 20, 2024.

National Governors Association Center for Best Practices & Council of Chief State School Officers. (2010). *Common Core State Standards for English language arts and literacy in history/social studies, science, and technical subjects*. Washington, DC: Authors. Accessed at https://learning.ccsso.org/wp-content/uploads/2022/11/ADA-Compliant-ELA-Standards.pdf on June 3, 2024.

Nelson, R. J. (2021) Podcasting services in academic libraries: A case study. *College and Undergraduate Libraries, 27*(2), 117–132.

OpenAI. (2023). *ChatGPT* (March 19 version) [Large language model]. Accessed at https://chat.openai.com/chat on March 19, 2024.

Paquet, S. (2002, October 1). *Personal knowledge publishing and its uses in research*. Accessed at https://radio-weblogs.com/0110772/stories/2002/10/03/personalKnowledgePublishingAndItsUsesInResearch.html on February 2, 2024.

Podcast. (n.d.). In *Oxford English Dictionary's online dictionary*. Accessed at www.oed.com/search/dictionary/?scope=Entries&q=podcast on May 20, 2024.

Present. (n.d.). In *Merriam-Webster's online dictionary*. Accessed at www.merriam-webster.com/dictionary/present on May 20, 2024.

Quoteresearch. (2019, March 1). *A work of art is never finished, merely abandoned*. Accessed at https://quoteinvestigator.com/2019/03/01/abandon on June 3, 2024.

Richardson, W. (2010). *Blogs, wikis, podcasts, and other powerful web tools for classrooms*. Thousand Oaks, CA: Corwin Press.

Sankey, M., Birch, D., & Gardiner, M. (2010) Engaging students through multimodal learning environments: The journey continues. *Proceedings ascilite Sydney*, 852–863.

Stille, S. (2011). Framing representations: Documentary filmmaking as participatory approach to research inquiry. *Journal of Curriculum and Pedagogy, 8*(2), 101–108.

Sturgis, C., Patrick, S., & Pittenger, L. (2011, July). *It's not a matter of time: Highlights from the 2011 competency-based learning summit*. Vienna, VA: International Association for K–12 Online Learning. Accessed at https://files.eric.ed.gov/fulltext/ED537332.pdf on February 2, 2024.

Tsang, A. (2017) Enhancing learners' awareness of oral presentation (delivery) skills in the context of self-regulated learning. *Active Learning in Higher Education, 21*(1), 39–50.

Utah State Legislature. (2021). *Personalized, competency-based learning grants program, Utah code 53F-5-501*. Accessed at https://le.utah.gov/xcode/Title53F/Chapter5/53F-5-S501.html on February 2, 2024.

Visible Learning. (2017). *Hattie ranking: 252 influences and effect sizes related to student achievement*. Accessed at https://visible-learning.org/hattie-ranking-influences-effect-sizes-learning-achievement/ on May 20, 2024.

Waldron, L. M., Covington, B., & Palmer, S. (2023): Critical pedagogy, counterstorytelling, and the interdisciplinary power of podcasts. *Journal of Curriculum and Pedagogy*. 1–19.

Woodson, J. (2014). *Brown girl dreaming*. New York: Puffin Books.

Woodson, J. [@JackieWoodson]. (2018, January 23). *I spent the morning with these beautiful young Ambassadors in their classroom in Salt Lake City, Utah. Their teacher is everything. This video is even more. I LOVE my job!! #Dreamers* [Post]. X. Accessed at https://x.com/JackieWoodson/status/955929484422623233?s=20 on March 22, 2024.

Woodward, J. (2022). Podcasting as pedagogy: Providing more than flexibility during challenging times. *Journal of Political Science Education, 18*(4), 614–623.

Zhang, H., Song, W., Shen, S., & Huang, R. (2014). The effects of blog-mediated peer feedback on learners' motivation, collaboration, and course satisfaction in a second language writing course. *Australasian Journal of Educational Technology, 30*(6).

# INDEX

## A

activities, list of
    copyright infringement or fair use, 20, 22, 23–24
    editing the fifteen-second film, 100–102
    everyone's a critic, 81–82, 84
    fifteen-second film festival, 102
    fifteen-second film project treatment, 85, 86
    internet safety vocabulary search, 20, 21
    one perfect pic, 93, 95
    screening your rough cut, 102
    shooting video and recording audio, 99–100
    shot styles scavenger hunt, 88–93
    storyboards, 93–94, 95, 96, 97
    ten facts about Cesar Chavez, 18–20
    writer of this poem, the, 27–28
    writing your script, 85, 87–88
A-roll footage, 83, 116, 129, 148
artificial intelligence (AI), 25
assessments and presentations, 15
audio recording
    activity: shooting video and recording audio, 99–100
    digital tools list, 26
    documentary short films and, 117–118
    music videos and, 147–148
    narrative short films and, 131
    podcasts and, 70, 72

## B

blog posts
    about, 34
    benefits of, 14–15
    conclusion, 43
    creators at work, 33–34
    digital projects, 36–43
    drafting, 38–40
    key features of, 34
    planning for, 36
    prewriting, 36–38
    proofreading, 42
    publishing, 42–43
    resources and exemplars for, 34
    revision, 40–41
    rubrics for, 35

Boolean operators, 18
breathing techniques, 56, 147
B-roll footage, 83, 116, 129, 148

## C

Canva, 26, 27, 30, 80, 103
ChatGPT-4, 25
class and student websites, 30
College and Career Readiness (CCR) anchor standards, 15–16
Common Core ELA standards, 13
copyright infringement and fair use
    activity: copyright infringement or fair use, 20, 22, 23–24
    music videos and, 139–140
critical friends
    about, 40–41
    critical friends feedback form, 41, 157
    documentary short films and, 119
    music videos and, 149
    narrative short films and, 133
    podcasts and, 73
    presentations and, 55–56

## D

digital tools and technology tips
    about, 25–26
    digital equipment sign-out sheet, 98
    digital project folders, 26
    digital tools list, 26
    mavens, 26–27, 29
    options, selecting, 29
    speech-to-text, 29
    translation tools, 29
digital videos. *See also* documentary short films; music videos; narrative short films
    about, 77
    amplifying student voices: online video-sharing platforms, 102–104
    benefits of video production, 77–79
    conclusion, 102–104
    digital tools list, 80
    film school, 79–102
    stages of video production, 79

digital voices. *See also* blog posts; podcasts; presentations; voice
    about, 13–14
    amplifying student voices, 29–31
    benefits of blogging, presentations, and podcasts, 14–17
    conclusion, 32
    digital tools and technology tips, 25–29
    online research, media literacy, and artificial intelligence, 17–25
documentary short films
    about, 106, 108
    benefits of video production, 78
    conclusion, 120
    creators at work, 105–106
    digital projects, 108–120
    planning for, 109
    postproduction, 118–120
    preproduction, 108–115
    production, 116–118
    resources and exemplars for, 108
    rubrics for, 107

## E

editing
    audio- and video-editing organizer, 146
    documentary short films and, 118–119
    music videos and, 148, 149
    narrative short films and, 132
    podcasts and, 73
empowerment, 1–2

## F

feedback
    critical friends and, 40–41
    feedback T-chart, 48
    presentations and, 57–58
    project-based learning and, 4
    types of, 48
fifteen-second film project. *See also* film school
    activity: editing the fifteen-second film, 100–102
    activity: fifteen-second film festival, 102
    activity: fifteen-second film project treatment, 85, 86
    examples of, 84
    planning page for, 85
    rubrics for, 82
    storyboards for, 96
film festivals, 102, 119, 133
film school
    about, 79–81
    digital tools list, 80
    postproduction, 100–102
    preproduction, 81–97
    production, 97–100
    production cues sheet, 99
    production roles sheet, 98–99
    resources and exemplars for, 79–80
    video production vocabulary sheet, 83
Freire, P., 16

## G

Google Scholar, 17
Google Sites, 30

## I

identity presentations, 27
infographics, 27
interviews. *See also* documentary short films; podcasts
    conducting interviews, 71, 117
    drafting interview questions, 70
    example interview request messages, 69, 112
    interview release form, 69
    types of, 113
introduction
    about kids as creators, 3
    benefits of digital projects, 4–6
    empowering student voices, 6
    engaging parents and school leaders, 6, 8
    how to use this book, 10

## L

large language models, 25
listening parties, 73
Lucas, G., 102

## M

media literacy, 22, 24–25
Media Literacy 101, 24
media release form examples, 8, 9
Meet the Media Monsters, 24
multimodal learning and the benefits of digital projects, 5–6
music videos
    about, 136, 138
    audio- and video-editing organizer, 146
    conclusion, 150–151
    creators at work, 135–136
    digital projects, 138–150
    drafting, 143–145
    lyrical outline, 141–142
    planning for, 139
    postproduction, 149–150
    preproduction, 138–145
    production, 145–149
    resources and exemplars for, 101–102, 138
    rubrics for, 137
    variations for, 151

## N

narration, 72, 100, 117–118, 131
narrative short films
    about, 122, 124
    conclusion, 133–134
    creators at work, 121–122
    digital projects, 124–133
    pitch sheet, 128
    planning for, 125
    postproduction, 131–133

preproduction, 125–129
production, 129–131
resources for, 124
rubrics for, 123
storyboards, 130
treatments for, 126
National Association for Media Literacy Education, 22
News and Media Literacy 101, 24–25

# O

online research. *See also* research
about, 17
activity: copyright infringement or fair use, 20, 22, 23–24
activity: internet safety vocabulary search, 20, 21
activity: ten facts about Cesar Chavez, 18–20
online search tools, 17–18
outlining, 39, 53, 54, 141–142

# P

parents, engaging parents and school leaders, 6, 8
peers. *See* critical friends
personalized, competency-based learning, 4–5
photography, principles of cheat sheet, 94. *See also* video recording and photography
phrase searching, 18
pitching
documentary short films, 111–112
narrative short film pitch sheet, 127–128
podcasts, 67–68
video production vocabulary sheet, 83
podcasts
about, 62, 64
benefits of, 16–17
common jobs, 70
conclusion, 74
creators at work, 61–62
digital projects, 64–74
intro and outro podcast organizer, 72
planning for, 65
podcasting platforms, 31
post-production, 73–74
preproduction, 65–70
production, 70–72
resources and exemplars for, 64
rubrics for, 63
postproduction. *See also* film school
about, 100
activity: editing the fifteen-second film, 100–102
activity: fifteen-second film festival, 102
activity: screening your rough cut, 102
documentary short films, 118–120
music videos, 149–150
narrative short films, 131–133
podcasts, 73–74
preproduction. *See also* film school

about, 81
activity: everyone's a critic, 81–82, 84
activity: fifteen-second film project treatment, 85, 86
activity: one perfect pic, 93, 95
activity: shot styles scavenger hunt, 88–93
activity: storyboards, 93–94, 95, 96, 97
activity: writing your script, 85, 87–88
documentary short films, 108–115
music videos, 138–145
narrative short films, 125–129
podcasts, 65–70
presentations
about, 46, 48–49
benefits of, 15–16
conclusion, 58–59
creators at work, 45–46
digital projects, 49–58
drafting, 53–55
identity presentations, 27
planning for, 50
prewriting, 50–52
proofreading, 56–57
publishing, 57–58
rehearsing and revising, 55–56
resources and exemplars for, 49
rubrics for, 47
variations for, 59
principles of photography cheat sheet, 94
production. *See also* film school
about, 97–98
activity: shooting video and recording audio, 99–100
documentary short films and, 116–118
music videos and, 145–149
narrative short films and, 129–131
podcasts and, 70–72
production cues sheet, 99
production roles sheet, 98–99
project-based learning (PBL), 4
public speaking, 15, 56
publishing
blog posts, 42–43
documentary short films, 119–120
music videos, 150
narrative short films, 133
podcasts, 74

# Q

QR codes
for documentary short film examples, 106, 110
for music video examples, 2, 136, 147
for narrative short film example, 122
for presentation example, 46

# R

reflection, after-project reflection reproducible, 158
relaxation techniques, 56

reproducibles for
    after-project reflection, 158
    critical friend feedback form, 157
    five fascinating facts form, 156
research. *See also* online research
    blog post prewriting, 38
    documentary preproduction, 112–114
    podcast preproduction, 68–69
    presentation prewriting, 52
    resources for, 17
role-play exercises, 56
rubrics
    blog posts and, 35, 40
    documentary rubric, 107
    fifteen-second film project rubric, 82
    music videos rubric, 137
    narrative film rubric, 123
    podcast rubric, 63
    presentations and, 47, 55–56

## S

screenplays and scripts
    activity: writing your script, 85, 87–88
    narrative short films, 125–128
    podcasts, 72
    presentations, 53, 55, 56–57
    short film screenplay template, 89
    video production vocabulary sheet, 83
site-specific searches, 18
slideshows, 59, 74, 120, 134, 151
sound effects, 73, 117–118, 131
speech-to-text, 29
storyboards
    activity: storyboards, 93–94, 95, 96, 97
    narrative short films preproduction, 129, 130
StudyCasts, 62. *See also* podcasts
synonym searching, 18

## T

toastmasters approach, 56
topic selection
    blog post prewriting, 37–38
    documentary preproduction, 109–110
    music video preproduction, 139–140
    podcast preproduction, 65–66
    presentation prewriting, 50–52
translation tools, 29
treatments
    activity: fifteen-second film project treatment, 85, 86
    documentary treatment writing, 111–112
    narrative short film treatment, 126
    podcast treatment writing, 67–68

## U

Utah State Board of Education media release form, 9

## V

video recording and photography
    activity: one perfect pic, 93, 95
    activity: shooting video and recording audio, 99–100
    activity: shot styles scavenger hunt, 88–93
    documentary shot list and editing organizer, 115
    principles of photography cheat sheet, 94
    shooting primary (A-Roll) and secondary (B-Roll) footage, 116–117, 129, 131, 148–149
    shot style cheat sheet, 90–91
Vimeo, 100, 103–104
vocal warm-ups, 147
voice. *See also* digital voices
    amplifying student voices, 29–31, 102–104
    embracing your own, 147–148
    empowering student voices, 6, 7

## W

webinars, 58
websites for class and students, 30
wildcard searches, 18
Woodson, J., 150
writer of this poem activity, the, 27–28

## Y

YouTube, 80, 102, 103

## Z

Zoom, 26, 58, 70–71, 80

### Making the Move With Ed Tech
*Troy Hicks, Jennifer Parker, and Kate Grunow*
Countless technology tools are available to teachers and coaches, but integrating technology in the classroom in a purposeful way is challenging. In this book, the authors cut through ed-tech jargon and frameworks to help you employ ed-tech tools strategically. Explore *moves*, or instructional strategies, both familiar and new, that facilitate student inquiry, dialogue, critical thinking, and creativity.
**BKG101**

### The Complete Guide to Blended Learning
*Catlin R. Tucker*
Skillfully shifting between online and in-person learning has become expected of teachers. In this essential guide, you will learn how to harness technology to enhance student learning in both realms. Combining theory, reflection, and personal experience, author Catlin R. Tucker equips educators with a wide variety of strategies and tools to support student and educator success in blended environments and beyond.
**BKG082**

### Connected Classrooms
*Beth Pandolpho*
Reimagine your school community. This practical guidebook will help you shift your mindset of online and blended learning from "backup plan" to unprecedented opportunity for rich connections and high-level learning. New and veteran teachers alike will gain insights for building in-person and online relationships with students and coworkers to achieve a learning community that supports social-emotional learning, equitable and inclusive instruction, and academic success.
**BKG075**

### Personalized Deeper Learning
*James A. Bellanca*
Foster deeper learning with two templates—one for students, the other for teachers—that increase student agency and learning transfer within critical skill sets. Any teacher—regardless of grade, existing curriculum, or student load—can adapt, scale, and sustain these powerful personalized learning plans. Chapters include driving questions, concrete strategies, helpful tool examples, playlists, sample rubrics, and more.
**BKF975**

### Motivated to Learn
*Staci M. Zolkoski, Calli Lewis Chiu, and Mandy E. Lusk*
Imagine a day in the classroom where you can devote all your energy to student learning instead of battling challenging behavior. In *Motivated to Learn*, you will gain evidence-based approaches for engaging students and equipping them to better focus in the classroom. With this book's straightforward strategies, you can learn to motivate all your students to actively participate in learning.
**BKG037**

Visit SolutionTree.com or call 800.733.6786 to order.

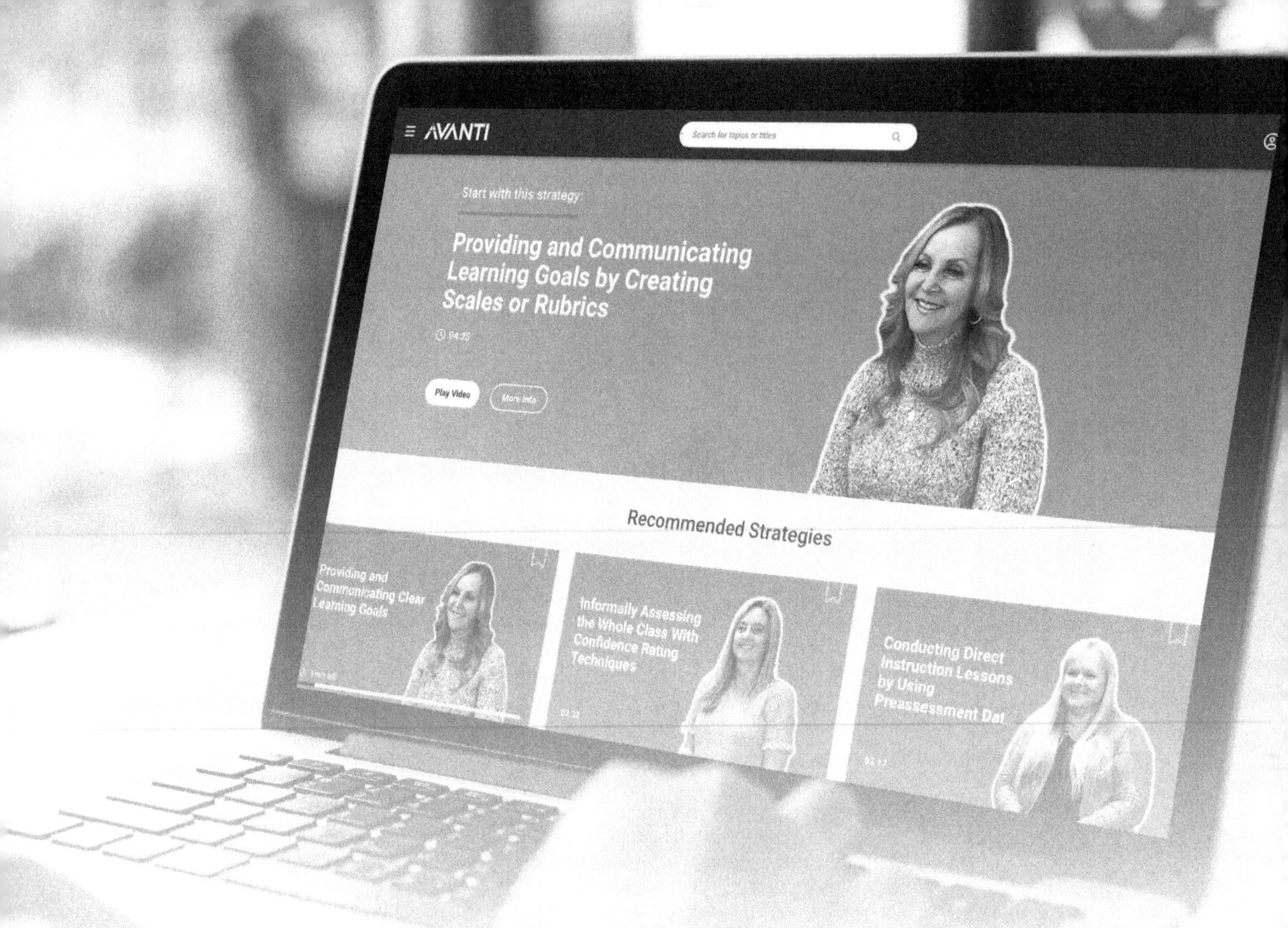

# AVANTI

## Grow your teacher toolkit by learning from other teachers

Take control of your professional growth and positively impact your students' lives with proven, ready-to-use classroom strategies. With Avanti, you'll get professional learning created by teachers, for teachers.

**Learn more**
My-Avanti.com/**GrowYourToolkit**